I pray you are blessed through the outpoured strength of my journey, because you are beloved.

— Jky

CONFESSIONS OF A
Butterfly:

Relationships, Food, and Self-Esteem

JESSICA KEY

Confessions of a Buddafli: Relationships, Food, and Self-Esteem

© 2017 Jessica Key

ISBN-13: 978-1981836895

ISBN-10: 1981836896

All rights reserved.

No part of this publication may be reproduced, stored in a retrieval system, stored in a database and / or published in any form or by any means, electronic, mechanical, photocopying, recording or otherwise, without the prior written permission of the publisher.

Cover photography: MD Willis Photography

www.buddainspired.com

You are more precious than I ever could have imagined. Your almond eyes remind me of my own the way they shine as the sunlight touches them. Your skin is as pure and smooth as your Egyptian grandmother. Your smile is as bright as the Son who died for you. I wrote this for you that you might know of my struggle and learn from my journey a better road to take.

I love you.

Contents

School Days 7
Senior to Freshman 17
Devin 29
Dirty Thirty 49
God said what? 57
Not so fast! 63
Love or Lust? 67
Live and Let Love 73

Poems

Chocolate Drops 6
Lives of Lily's 16
Lost and Never Found 20
Sacrifice 21
Nubian Goddess 30
He Loved Me 31
Last Night 35
I Don't Like You 41
Alone 43
Waiting 44
The Weekend 49
More Than 59
Past Life 84

Chocolate Drop

If you ever met her you would swear that we were twins. We were two chocolate drops manufactured in the same chocolate factory. We were simply beautiful, shining in the Son never melting in his brightness only becoming sweeter and sweeter by the day.

I was her little chocolate drop. And as a child every time I came home from school discouraged from bullies and life itself she would wipe my tears away and say, "it's okay my little chocolate drop." Somehow that always seemed to make me feel better. My mom always knew just what to say to take the hurt away even if only for a moment. My life always felt like living when I was in the arms of my mom. If only, I could stay there.

School Days

I was born in Little Rock, Arkansas, on September 24, 1983, to Valerie and Calvin Key Sr. at St. Vincent Infirmary. The funny thing is, I was supposed to be Jesse but to my parent's surprise, that day Jessica Lynn Key was born. And I was as chocolate as I could be with a head full of hair as I came from my mother's womb. I can't say for sure, but I think I immediately fell in love with my mom once I saw her face.

I was the third and final child birthed between my mother and father, and I think anyone who met me could tell I was the baby of the family. I pretty much got away with everything and was spoiled by everyone in my household. My mom told me that once I started talking, my older brother, Calvin Jr., stopped talking. Apparently, I talked enough for the both of us: can you imagine? The envy of my eye growing up however, was my older sister, Melissa. She was so beautiful and surprisingly enough—with as dark as I was—she was light skinned. As a kid, I don't think I

8

knew what a complexion was; all I knew was that my sister was gorgeous and I wasn't.

As children, we don't truly notice how different we are from one another until it is pointed out. The first time I even started to realize I was "different" was when a boy at school complimented me by saying, "You look just like your sister, but you're black." This happened just as I was transitioning into the sixth grade. Honestly, if I knew what was in store for me beyond that very comment I would have preferred being home schooled rather than walking through the doors of Dunbar Middle School as a chubby little black girl.

I have nothing but fond memories of elementary school, however I can't say the same for junior high. I guess you can say that middle school is when my life really began. If it wasn't for my mom, I don't think I would have ever made it out alive. Although I loved my dad dearly, there was just something about my mom that made my troubles melt away when I saw her. She always wanted me to know that I was beautiful and would often put me in front of a mirror and make me point out my "beautiful" features. She would hold my face in her hands and kiss my cheeks explaining to me how beautiful my almond eyes were and how pretty my smile was. My mom always knew how to make me feel better when I was down, and often called me her little chocolate drop.

In reality, momma's little chocolate drop was 196 pounds in the sixth grade. Although I've always been tall, I still had one of the

roundest faces in the world, at least that was my perspective. As I transitioned into junior high, I was introduced to "roasting." Back in 1996, "roasting" was the word used when multiple people would talk about someone for laughs. Apparently, the better you were at making people laugh about another's imperfections, the funnier you were considered to be.

Unfortunately, I was terrible at this and never even tried to succeed at it. As far as I can remember, I was humiliated every other day by some of my classmates. I never understood why boys were always so mean to me, let alone why the pretty girls always seemed to find time to join in. Once I found out that one of the boys that talked about me the most actually had a crush on me. I was totally confused that a guy could dedicate his life to making my life miserable and all the while have a crush on me. He used to call me Smokey the Bear and tell me that *only I could prevent forest fires*. Although this phrasing may have been and still may be funny to some it was certainly not funny to me. Can you imagine walking down a hallway and hearing the kids yell, "Smokey, Smokey?" I found myself secretly crying most evenings and looking at myself in the mirror thinking why did I have to be so black and ugly. I just didn't understand why I couldn't be light skinned and pretty like my sister.

Sticks and stones may break my bones,

But words will never hurt me.

Who created this saying? Whoever it was couldn't possibly have ever heard a guy whispering, "She is so fat!" "She is as

black as tar!" "Smokey, come here I'm on fire!" They must have never heard a girl whisper, "Oh, I'm so glad I'm not black like her!" "Ugh, I am so glad I don't look like Jessica!" Words are powerful, and without them I don't think we would exist. I believe it was God who spoke us into existence. "Let there be light." And there was light. Without words, how could a man ask a woman to marry him? Without words, how could a woman say yes? Words are the foundation of our very existence, and they are influential so we must be careful what we speak out loud. As a kid, I wished someone could've taught all the bullies of the world that one simple fact. But time may have been better spent building the self-esteem of little girls that looked like me. Although roasting was a daily routine that I endured, I remained sweet and often would help those who talked about me with their work if they needed it. I was raised to be kind to others because you would want them to be kind to you. It wasn't a matter of playing suck-up or wanting brownie points; it was a matter of something I still believe in to this day—treating others with dignity and respect.

I must admit that at my lowest moments I contemplated suicide and even attempted it on more than one occasion. I felt that it was better for me to no longer be here on earth than to continue to cry myself asleep some nights. Looking back now, I am thankful that the attempts to take my own life were interrupted on each occasion. As I look back now, I am deeply saddened that I allowed myself to get so low in life that I actually thought to end my own life.

10

Low times like these are why I embraced emotional eating. I believe it was in junior high that food ultimately became my best friend. It was the only thing that made any sense to me. It was available when I needed it, and it never had an issue playing any role in my life at any point or time. As the school years continued, I began to look at myself in the mirror and notice just how ugly I really was. I actually started to believe all the things that were said to me in class. There would be some days in which I would simply stare in the mirror and cry at the horror I saw. Although there were days when I could almost see what my mother saw in me, those days were few and far between. I still felt like a little fat, black girl.

It wasn't until I began writing my feelings down one day that I discovered something I loved more than food. Poetry. I started writing poetry every day and even began to write poems for other people on special occasions. This was my release. I wrote for days on end and even filled a few diaries with just poems. Some days I even managed to find my smile in the mirror and see a bit of beauty in it. I think I was starting to be okay with my reflection, and it must have started to show on the outside because I finally got my first boyfriend at the end of my seventh-grade year.

He wasn't like all the other boys, and I had known him for years at church. I had arrived...and I fell head over heals for PJ. He was a sweetheart and a wonderful kisser. Can you believe that I finally got kissed? After what felt like decades, a boy met me and was nice to me and wanted to walk around holding my hand. Oh,

11

how I never thought the day would come. He was perfect, just perfect for me, and I loved him all the more as the days went on. The only problem with PJ was that he didn't go to my school. So no matter how comfortable and how happy he made me feel, that happiness only came when I was able to see him at church.

Luckily for me I was COGIC and we were in church all the time. If you don't know what COGIC is, it stands for Church of God in Christ. This is also another way of saying I was brought up Pentecostal, and I was at church Sunday through Saturday. COGIC was serious about having church on multiple days of the week, especially if there was a revival going on. As I look back over my life, I can definitely say that I am thankful for the way I was brought up. I accepted the love and salvation of Jesus Christ in my life at the early age of 11. So over the last 20-plus years of my life, I have known the presence of God.

Having a personal relationship with God brought me through so many things over the years. He watched over me through all the pain and sadness of being talked about and judged. And as a 12-year-old, I felt that finding PJ was a gift from God.

Although we got to see one another over the summer, by the time the fall semester of eighth grade came along I was right back to my normal reality. Food once again replaced my sweetheart and held my hand in his absence.

I guess my mom saw the "fruit" of this secondary relationship and wasn't very happy with it, because one day she came home from

work, saw me sitting on the couch eating chips and said, "You are going to play volleyball this year." Of course, this statement caught me off guard, and I immediately asked, "Why?"

"Because you're a couch potato; you're just sitting here eating and feeding your face. And your little face is getting rounder and rounder."

So, that year I began playing volleyball in an effort to increase my daily physical activities. I can't really say that I was good at volleyball, but at least I tried. And more importantly, my mom was happy that I was doing more than eating chips on the couch every day. The following school year, I played volleyball again. My mom was really intent on keeping me active.

I can't say that much changed about me other than gaining a few more friends that played on the team. However, one of the darkest times of my life did come around my ninth grade year. Growing up my parents often allowed me to have friends over that spent the night. One friend in particular came over quite often. We had a lot of fun together, however one night changed all that.

As I look back now I feel like I should have stopped her or I should have yelled for my parents to come in and save me but for some reason I didn't.

Honestly, I had never experienced anything like it before, and I didn't really know what was happening. It was as if time froze. All I knew was that she touched me in a place I had never been

13

I know it may seem foolish, but I literally just didn't know what was going on. As a child who grew up going to church, we never discussed sex, rape, molestation, masturbation or anything of the sort. So as a 13-year-old girl being touched by another girl, I felt awkward and completely confused. It wasn't until writing this book 21 years later that I even told my family what happened to me as a child.

I just didn't want to deal with the shame or the emotions that came with being molested. Hell, I didn't even realize that's what had happened until years later when I learned what the word truly meant.

I just decided to move on and keep that part of my life to myself. Besides, wasn't it my fault for not stopping her or for not yelling for someone to help me?

15

Lives of Lily's

So many secrets hidden and buried deep
So many hurts have been left with me
Little black girls touched by other boys
Little black boys touched by other black men
Girls touching girls that have been touched by others
The secret lives of lily's spread quietly.
Across the field and into the air no one tells of the hurts
they've endured
Across the fields and into the trees your secret is safe
with me
Body shaming and being shamed of the things that
have been left with us
Hurts and pains and only we hold the blame
Never telling or understanding why it happened to me
Secretly sad, openly smiling
Hidden places made public
Teary eyes wiped clean

Senior to Freshman

Well, it was time for me to move on and forward in my life. My hurts, my shame, and my feelings had been hidden away and there was no time to cope or to deal with what happened. I just buried it down deep inside my soul and carried on. Before I knew it, junior high passed me by; what seemed like an eternity was only three years. Next thing you know, I looked up and my mom and I were at John L. McClellan High School registering me for school. By this time, I had decided that I would start high school as Lynn (my middle name). I decided that I would change who I was and be cool this time around. I would be so confident that no one would ever dare to talk about me. I was ready for the big league!

Well, apparently a large majority of my junior high classmates followed me to McClellan, so Lynn was out the door and Jessica was back. Amazingly enough, high school was easier for me. I really found my own personality and let it shine. I had finally

blossomed. I even had a group of male friends that I casually flirted with and it was reciprocated. I think I had finally become OK with being a chubby, little black girl. I think I even embraced it. Later in my senior year, I was actually voted biggest flirt and most talented by my senior class.

As great as all that sounds, there was still one small, underlying issue. I was 296 pounds in the 11th grade.

At this point, my mom decided that it was time the entire household lost some weight. For the next few months, we were going to be doing the Atkins diet. Breakfast, lunch and dinner all became meat and veggies. While at school, my friends would look at me crazy as I walked through the halls with a bag of broccoli and a small container of ranch dip. I actually loved the diet. My mom told me I could eat all the food I wanted as long as it was meat or a vegetable. That was like winning the lottery, because I got to eat all the time.

I still felt on top of the world because in high school, no one really talked about me. I was free to just be Jessica, unapologetically. That is until Leon P. reminded me of my size one day in chemistry class. Leon was actually one of the boys I occasionally flirted with on a daily basis. We were friends and often found ourselves laughing together and having many random conversations. It never even crossed my mind that he was actually attracted to me until one day in class when he let the cat out of the bag.

We were partnered up in groups and laughing as usual about whatever the hot topic of the week was at the time. After he told

a joke. I threw my head back laughing and when I looked back up at him he had this sincere look on his face; I asked what was wrong. Leon then looked deep into my eyes and said, "If you were just a little bit smaller I would go out with you."

Honestly I don't remember what my response was to him. I've racked my brain over the years and the only thing I could come up with is that I probably said, "OK." I mean, what do you say to something like that? Ironically, this was the year of the Atkins diet and that year I lost 36 pounds. And just to clarify, no, I didn't start dating Leon.

Luckily for me, I still had PJ. We held on to each other through high school and he never had an issue with my size. Maybe that's why it was so easy to give him my virginity like it was a piece of candy. I didn't really know its value at the time. All I knew was that this was the first boy who was OK with what I saw in the mirror every day for 16 years.

Tuesday, July 8, 2000, still feels like yesterday. I believe the time was 2:34 p.m. That day at the tender age of 16, I lost my virginity to my first boyfriend. I followed him up the stairs, and as we entered his sister's bedroom I didn't even know what to expect. I don't know if he undressed me or if I undressed myself. I just lay there like a mannequin as still and quiet as a church mouse. I didn't know what to think or what to do. All I know is that I just wanted to be with him in that moment. He was happy, and to me that was all that really mattered. I felt honored that he chose to be a part of my life. I felt blessed that he was OK with

Lost and Never Found

You ever lose yourself in someone and never even
know it until you look back and see that your
reflection looks a lot like there's?
Every time I think I've found someone to pour
myself into I end up losing the reality of me because
of the infatuation of he.
You do things just because you care;
making sacrifices outside yourself to please them
with the hopes of having love returned.
To just lie there next to someone and know what

forever.
I didn't notice until years later after being in relationship after relationship that this was a very defining moment for me. The moment that I subconsciously decided to be someone that would please a man at all cost, even if it meant giving up my most prized possession. To lay down with a man just to make him happy would become my mode of operating, and for years to come this would be my struggle.

Sacrifice

My body has been my sacrifice to men for years
I have given it with no hopes of it ever being returned
In exchange I hoped to receive love and companionship but the only thing ever given back was indignant thank yous and pain
I've felt the need to share my graceful gift of virtue to pour myself like a picture of freshly squeezed orange juice into the lives of hopeless men full of potential
I allowed them to enter into my cocoon and plant ails them; and that they are better because of your presence is amazing
But what then becomes of you?
As you lay there soaked in the loneliness of him there is nothing that can be said to make you feel differently.
To share pains and pleasures, let downs and uplifting moments, secrets and whispers would only appear to be forced and unreal.
So you just pretend that happiness lies in bed as you lay in bed with yet another.

seeds of internalization and alienation
All the while what I gained was nothing.
While there they awake the sensations of my body,
which made me to fall in love
I stayed only to be abused mentally, emotionally, and
God forbid physically but it happened every time I
laid just because he wanted or I needed to please him
My life was stolen,
My mind was taken over by the theory of please a
man to keep a man
You know that old saying of Lay, Stave, and ask no
questions and he'll eventually stay
By definition a real relationship is based on
commitment on both parts and most importantly
communication
How can you ever know what I need or even begin to
understand my existence without getting to know me
If we never interact on a vertical level, horizontal will
cripple us,
So allow me, no, let me bring you into a world full of
conversation and elation reached through sensational
thoughts of words expressed phenomenally
Let me bring you into my world, a world created

to formulate and originate a real man, someone unafraid to be loved, held, and nurtured. Welcome to a world where a man is unafraid to love me and share the world with me as his own.

So here I was a new woman. After having lost my virginity, I thought things would be different for me but I still found myself to be unhappy. Having sex didn't change me the way I thought it would. I thought for sure that it would give me this strength or this cosmic power that would allow joy to shower down upon my spirit and make all of my sorrows disappear.

I was wrong.

In my mind, I was still a fat, black, and soon-to-be 12th grader. I decided it was time that I started planning for my future. Although I made good grades throughout my high school years, my ACT scores weren't scholarship material. The only thing I had going for me outside of my grade-point average was my voice. Since I sang in the choir at church my entire life, and sang in the choir at school, I decided to talk to my choir teacher about applying for music scholarships. He recommended that I audition for Philander Smith College. He worked with me throughout the first semester of my senior year and prepared me for my audition in the Spring. Who would have thought that

23

singing "Amazing Grace," one time would pay for college? I received my scholarship and couldn't have been happier. I was on my way to college.

By the time graduation came around I had ballooned up to 303 pounds. But I was headed to college and promised myself I would reinvent my life all over again. I decided I wasn't going to be the fat, black girl anymore. I was ready.

Lucky for me, no one cared about how I looked in college so this let me off the hook for changing my eating habits. Once school started in August of 2001, I pretty much became a robot for the next four years. I was still living at home with my parents, and I would just go to school, work and go home. That is, until my life was changed forever one Friday night in 2005.

I got a phone call from an old high school classmate of mine that was heading to a poetry venue called Mediums. She said that it was the place to be on Friday nights in Little Rock. Since I literally had nothing to do, I decided to join her that night and see for myself.

So we both got all jazzed up and went to Mediums, and to my surprise another old high school classmate was the host of the event. He asked me if I wanted to sign up to do some poetry because he remembered I wrote poems back in school. I said yes, and he told me I needed to come up with a stage name. I thought about it for only one second and wrote down Buddafli, and told him to pronounce it as butterfly but with "d's."

I decided to own who I was, a unique caterpillar destined for change. I'd always loved the story of how butterflies came to exist and decided to embrace it as my poetry name. When he finally called me to the stage, I recited my poem and the entire room loved it. It was like no one noticed my size or the color of my skin. All they noticed was my talent. It was amazing. And I knew at that very moment that Mediums would be my new safe haven.

Over the next five years, I blossomed in ways I never thought I would. I became confident and felt sexy all at the same time. It was truly because of the acceptance I felt whenever I walked through the doors of Mediums. Funny enough, there were even what I considered 'pretty girls' who told me they were jealous of me. Can you believe it? A pretty girl being jealous of big ol' chocolate me. All because of my stage presence? How could this be true?

Because of my popularity, I got booked to perform poetry at places across the state and even the country. I performed in various cities including Little Rock, Conway, Fayetteville, Memphis, Atlanta, Dallas and Hollywood. Yes, I went all the way to Hollywood and performed at BB King's. My life became something to talk about.

Meanwhile, I wasn't able to stay in my shoes for as long as I would have liked to during a 30-minute poetry set. Due to my weight, my feet would hurt and I would end up taking them off. It was time for me to make a change in my life.

25

So, I hired a personal trainer and over the next three months, I lost about over 20 pounds and got down to 276. I felt better and most importantly, I could stay in my shoes longer. As time went on, I ended up leaving my personal trainer and decided to do things on my own. As you can imagine, I was not successful in doing so and before I knew it, I was back up to 286.

It wasn't until September of 2009 that I joined an actual boot camp that made a huge impact on my life. My best friend suggested I try out a trainer by the name of Kameelah Harris, owner of WOW Fitness. She said that it would really benefit me to be with someone like Kameelah because of her personality. Little did I know that once I met Kameelah, I would fall in love with not only her personality but also the way she cared for her clients. She was truly something special, and I'm thankful to have her as a trainer and as a friend almost nine years later.

I truly was dedicated to working out with Kameelah. She held 5 a.m. boot camps every morning. Monday through Thursday I would find myself somehow making it out of bed to go and run up and down a hill; sometimes I would even have to carry her up the hill on my back. I wanted a change. I needed a change. And this was it. I wanted to be free from caring about how other people felt about me. I wanted to feel love through the eyes of myself based on what I was doing for myself, not necessarily what was happening on the outside. Don't get me wrong, I loved that my body was changing but even more than that, I was beginning to love how my mindset was changing. Though I still had ups and

downs, I felt like I was getting to a place where I didn't need a man to define my beauty or my worth.

That is until..........

28

Devin

It was the way Devin took care of me and brought me soup when I was sick and even asked how my day was over the phone -- and not just through a text message. It seems silly to think that that's all it took for me to fall head over heels in love with a man at the age of 29. But it was more than that. It was the way he looked out for me, the way he always had something to say about the men I dated and how they were all wrong for me. He cared. He cared about more than what lay between my legs or how many cups my chest could fill. He cared about me. He wasn't like all the others, or so I thought.

Though we never once kissed or even held hands as our friendship grew, I often found myself imagining what sex with him would be like.

I thought he would gently place one hand on my left shoulder while touching my chin and lifting my lips to his. I thought he would undress me and allow me to see his eyes delighted as each

enlarged breast left my bra falling south to land quickly on my enlarged front. I felt he would make me feel as if my size was never a problem to him. I thought he'd lay me down and slowly enter into my domain while asking if I was OK. I thought that if we ever crossed that friendship line, it would be magical and for days I'd write poems inspired by my experience.

Nubian Goddess

Beautiful slanted eyes that steal your soul
with one glance
Dimpled cheeks that capture your heart at one glimpse
Accented brows that are covered in pits of
shallow chocolate skin
Confidence of a lioness beginning to stock its prey
Elegance of a doe in the forest drinking
from the fountain
Hips that move as smoothly as the
glide of an eagles wings
Up and down and up swiveling constantly with the
rhythms of the music that encamps inside her soul
He emasculates her with a mere glance of
his deeply rooted Nigerian eyes
Grabbing her wrist while trying to bend her to his will
Wanting nothing more than to make her
his African Queen

he Loved Me

He said he loved the handles of my love and the
curves of my torso.

He said my thickness was never a problem and
that I should learn to accept my beauty, deal with
it, embrace it, and live the life of a woman who is
aware of her rolls of chocolate sunshine that add
to the vivaciousness of every piece of clothing that
touches her body.

He also said that the number on my scale didn't
reflect the largeness of my heart. And that my
beauty was beyond the pounds that clouded my
ex's mind.

This guy filled my head with thoughts that had
long been cast into the shadows of my soul, a soul
that trembled and hid inside of a body neglected by
real love and bombarded by counterfeit lovers.

His name was poetry and he told me he loved my
smile and that if I were ever to change to never lose
the gift of bringing sunshine to this dark place we
call the world.

This P O E T R Y filled me with feelings and
emotions that opened me up to see the loveliness of
a face in the mirror that was never recognized as
my own.

He even told me he loved the dimple in my right

I was wrong.

After a five-year friendship of never even as much as a kiss on the cheek, Devin and I slept together and it was nothing like I dreamed.

June 11, 2013, around 10:17 p.m., I remember putting on a mixture of blue and pink eye shadow creating an illusion of purple. Slipping on a fuchsia skirt and a navy blue blouse, I topped it all off with blue velvet, five-inch pumps. Baby, you

cheek the one that I'd always hoped no one would notice.

He told me to never stop breathing words of wisdom into the generation that was beneath me and to strip myself of all insecurities that had been in belted into my spirit.

He told me not to be ashamed of childhood scars and bruises from past relationships because he too had been scarred.

He loved on my essence and kissed my being inside and outside sideways and backwards until an orgasm of rhythmic words burst from within bringing forth the life of a child called Acceptance.

couldn't tell me nothing, I was fine as wine, honey! I hit the River Market District of Little Rock and not soon after, finding a seat in a crowded club, I got a phone call. It was Devin.

He said, "I see you lighting up the town in your bright colors." Of course, I immediately looked around to find him but was sadly disappointed to see he was not in the club. I thought he was out of town, so the call was definitely a surprise. He quickly told me that he had just arrived downtown and caught a glimpse of me as he headed to get food from a nearby restaurant.

He asked, "When are you heading home?"

With a slight giggle in my voice at the thought of being able to see him that night, I stated, "Whenever you tell me to." (For some reason this made me feel as though I was really somebody. He called me of all people. I must be special.)

He stated, "I'll see you at your place in twenty."

Honey, that was all I needed. I ditched my friends as if I was a newborn playing with toys and suddenly got a scent of momma's milk. I was gone! He needed me, so I had to stop everything I was doing in order to be fully available to give him whatever it was that he wanted.

And thus followed the shattered dreams of how my first time with Devin really went.

That night I lay next to him in nothing but white socks, a spaghetti strapped black tank and a black thong. After having

33

already had a heaping portion of fellatio, he put a condom on and told me he was ready to have sex. I let him know that I loved him and he replied the same. I said that things would change once we crossed this line and he simply said, "I'm ready."

He positioned me on my stomach and didn't even take my panties off. I had to do that myself. He slowly yet aggressively thrust himself inside me. I suppose I should have been happy that he chose to share himself with me, but I wasn't. I saw no sparks, no fireworks, no sunrise, not even a bird singing outside my window. Afterwards, I lay there trying to hold back the tears. I didn't let one tear out. I thought to myself, "What's done is done and there is no sense in crying now."

Although he spent the night, there were no words spoken until the morning came and he prepared to leave.

He said, "Give me your pinky."

Confused at first, I hesitated and he said it again.

"Give me your pinky."

So, I reached my pinky out to him and he grabbed it only to say, "Pinky swear that you'll never tell anyone we slept together."

I agreed and then walked him to the door. My heart had just been ripped out and cut into pieces. But I understood. He didn't want anyone to know. I mean, it was our business and no one else's. Who needs to know anyway? No one? right? Just us.

Last Night

Last night I unleashed my soul to you.
I opened up my legs and spread my wings as I watched
myself wrap my arms around you and call out your
name.
I was astonished, amazed, and speechless.
My body had let go of its sanity and my mind took a
break from reality.
I let you unleash something inside of me filled with hurt
and pain, confusion, and blame.
I let you inside of me.
Inside of more than my body.
Inside my mind, my being, my heart, and within those
moments inside of these hours, my inner parts, were
pushed way back inside of me and my thoughts were
bundled and cramped into an unreachable place.
I was outside of myself.
I was on the other side of reason,
And then,
And then, you stopped, you explained how he had
a mind of his own and as I lay there holding myself
and contemplating on what the next move would be
what the next step could be what the next day would

bring your sincerity entered into my ear as you asked
the simple question.
Are you okay?
Are you okay because you see I know that it has been a
long time for you and I know that you are a bit uneasy
that's why I took it easy.
And I laughed at the thought of you jumping up and
down inside of me barely hard as you explained
being easy.
Watching you hold my legs and brace your arms
around my limbs I was dumbfounded thinking what
if anything can I do to let him know he's piercing
more than what appears in this midnight thong more
than what he sees in this shirt.
He is taking and reshaping the very essence of me,
As we lay there both tired and breathless,
sleep falls upon u,
As the early morning rises upon us I feel you leave to
relieve yourself and return needing to relieve yourself,
And again I lay as submissive as a pet poodle born to
his mother I lay there allowing you to dog me and slide
me and ride me and run me to the ends of the earth.
As I lay there I am overwhelmed by your touch by your
assertive nature to take charge and lead me to a place

*the first cut of meat from Tuesday's market,
of submission uncovered by latex, free, and as raw as*
*As I lay there on my knees hunched over in your
arms a part of me realizes that this is what I wanted.
To give myself to you reasonless, to let you have a piece
of my body to let you enjoy a piece of my soul.
I realize that I wanted to feel you inside of me that I
wanted to break my celibacy,
Not because you deserved it but because.
I realize that there was not a reason for me to lay
with you,
No reason for me to exploit my body for counterfeit
kisses and bogus hugs,
I realize that I was the magician that orchestrated this
entire disaster and as I lay here confused and booed up
with you I remember,
I remember that it is only a facade and a mirage of
what I wish to come true someday,
I realize that my dream of laying and playing and
toying with my man have been decapitated by the
meaningless time that I have spent with you not getting
to know you but placing band aids on broken legs and
washing broken hearts with shredded towels.
I realize that the night we spent together was for naught*

and now time goes on and to belong to you or even to lay with you again is a thought and a desire unwanted.

Looking back, I realize now that any man who would ask you to be his secret wants to keep you from growing and flourishing. It's like purchasing a flower and putting it in a room with no lights and no windows. In life I've realized that it's up to me to escape the room and seek the light I so desperately need. I can't be afraid to let it touch me and pull me out of the darkness.

I really wish I could say, after that moment, I found the light that I needed to escape the darkness. I wish I could say after that moment I came to and realized that I deserved more than what was being offered. But I can't. That day, I made a choice to settle. I made a choice to start a sexual relationship with the hopes of it becoming more than that in the future. The crazy thing is, there was never a time in which a relationship was discussed.

Not once did Devin ever say, "I want us to be more than what we are," or "I want to make you mine so that no one can claim you as their own."

These were simply all the thoughts that ran through my mind on a daily basis. I thought that surely if I sucked, fucked and swallowed enough, while making myself available at every waking moment of the day, it would be enough.

Unfortunately, it was never enough.

I continued to sleep with Devin, but I had a plan. I acquired my own little boy toy to keep my mind occupied, Trevor. Haven't we all done that before? You sleep with someone who is no where near boyfriend material but is capable of scratching the itch you have for the moment as you wait for the one you truly want to reciprocate the feeling. I thought it was a great plan that would keep me centered. I really wanted to stop sleeping with Devin, but somehow I wasn't strong enough to leave him alone. But when I was with my "friend," it gave me some warped sense of balance. Although I still yearned for Devin, I was in control of my feelings and wasn't sitting around waiting on him to make me his girlfriend. It wasn't until February of 2014 that I even began to realize that I needed to truly leave Devin alone.

It's crazy how as I look back on all my hardships and pains in life and realize that each instance was followed by an in-depth passion for food. It seemed as though food was always the answer to the stress I had in life. Although I thought I had gained control over my emotional eating habits after working hard with Kameelah to drop 60 pounds, I realized that it took me five years to lose that weight. Because I always went back to old unhealthy habits when life hit hard. Throughout those five years, I had so many ups and downs, turnovers and upsets that my weight fluctuated as much as my relationships did. By 2014, I weighed in at 234, and it looked great on me.

Too bad all that would change in one night.

39

February 11, 2014, I was wearing some black three-inch pumps with my legs rubbed down and calf's shinning like the sun as the clouds burst to let him through. I wore a short, black mini-dress with a pearl necklace and earrings to match. I had taken the time to twist my hair into a French role and put on a minimum amount of makeup. Weeks earlier, Devin had given me tips on what to wear and what not to wear. I thought my outfit was perfect. It was just enough me sprinkled with a dash of him. It wasn't until a few hours into his birthday dinner that I discovered he had a girlfriend. This is the moment I went into cardiac arrest. By now, we had been sleeping together for over a year, and I had no idea he was dating someone.

All the time we spent together and all the midnight calls still meant nothing. I played myself. Somewhere deep inside, I had convinced myself that I could handle a relationship based purely on sex. I had convinced myself that I was savvy enough to get a man to commit to me over time. Initially, I knew he loved me as a friend and I thought he was falling in love with my ability to please him. I thought, surely the next step would be a relationship. I mean why wouldn't he want to commit to me?

That night:

Devin quieted the room and gently placed his hand on her shoulder and professed his love and admiration for her in front of his closest friends and more importantly, in front of me. I watched her smile and blush with embarrassment and glee. She was elated to be proclaimed his woman, his lover, and his prize.

At that moment I felt like saying:

I Don't Like You

Not until today did I realize why it is that....

I don't like you.

Why every time I see you I get disgusted and can't stand yo bustedness,

Why every time I hear your voice it irritates me till I can't sleep or eat any more,

At dinner it vibrates twice and rings through the echoes of my soul

I...don't...Like...YOU....

For there is something about you that makes me roll my eyes and clean my nose

Something that makes me want to regurgitate you into a field of hungry mice so that they could eat you alive

There is something that tears at me when I see your pretty little nose and slightly slanted eyes

I don't like you

Your smile isn't true

It hides being jealous of me as I enter into a room

It shivers at the sound of my name and
my very existence
Your mood is swayed, your speech is slurred
Your thoughts transformed from their original form
Your walk moved to the right as you look at me
I don't like you
And until today I didn't realize that it's because,
I'm sleeping with your man

But I didn't. Instead, I just smiled. I even managed to hug him and tell her she did a fabulous job standing by his side.

Once I exited the building, my face exploded. I could barely breathe and my eyes were swelling shut from the enlarged tears that filled them. Did I forget to mention that I had the pleasure of capturing the entire event on camera? Oh, what a joy to be able to push rewind and see your heart being trampled on over and over again. I didn't need the footage though, because the events of that night were embedded into my brain and repeatedly played over and over again.

That night, I literally screamed myself to sleep thinking of how foolish I had been to not realize he'd found someone by now. I should have known that I was his secret because I wasn't good enough to be his girlfriend.

43

Here I lay alone in a bed covered in the color of roses thinking to myself who loves me and who really cares

After passing out from the tears, I finally managed to wake up and gather enough strength to turn my phone back on. And of course, he had left a message. I called with the intent of giving him a piece of my mind, but instead I found myself listening to him explain the fact that he told me he was dating someone. After wanting to hurl myself out of a window, I simply said, "I need a break." He was devastated and apologetic to the point of tears. I explained how I was not that kind of girl, and if I had known that he was in a committed relationship, I never would have started sleeping with him.

A few days later, I invited him over and explained that it was never my intention to begin this affair with him, that I had decided to seek counseling for various reasons, and that I needed his support in this effort. He proclaimed that he was willing to do whatever it took to ensure my happiness. Three days later, we had sex and in some distorted way, I thought that this was the day in which I gained control over my life. I knew he had a girlfriend, but obviously he didn't "really" mean all the things he said the night of the party because he was with me, right? It was now my decision to continue seeing him but only when I wanted to make the time. I was in control, right?

Waiting

I'm waiting for a love that is a triple chocolate caramel macchiato covered in masculinity and unafraid of a better tomorrow.

In a world full of fonnies and fens I stand here honest, open and sincere about my desire to be wanted and my need to be held and if nothing else to be admired from afar and adored in person

I cry sometimes at the thought of being hurt another day, another time, after the thought of being used as a mistress passes through my thoughts

I realize it is all a dream and I have yet to enter into the reality of a relationship based on trust, real commitment and a desire to be with someone who is giving, caring and truthful in all aspects of life
Life something that is not to be taken lightly but lived in a way that allows you to look back and say

I lived my life as a result of myself, my needs and my hope of a better future for my soul

So now I leave you and I shall go to sleep with four pillows a fitted sheet and a blanket and a wish for a better tomorrow.

strong black woman
a love that is real and untainted, true and
honest honorable and faithful, caring and
understanding, deep and unwavering,
fulfilling and resilient
A love that knows how to take the aggressive role as I
ever so nervously take the passive one allowing my soft
side to shine through and the independent one
to take a back seat
I'm waiting for a love that will have me reading recipe
books to challenge my skills in the kitchen to make sure
he can be satisfied and pleased in every way possible
A love that will anticipate my mood as the rain falls
and prepare for my attitude as the sun rises
I'm waiting for a love that can appreciate my beauty
and Nubian ways and is comfortable sharing me with
a room full of men because he knows I am coming
home to him
A love that will rush home to see the new payless
pumps and anxiously await the fashion show
A love that has a sense of humor and can laugh when
my joke flops terribly but also lift me up when life drops
hard on me
A love that doesn't have to be told what to or how to do

but knows where his place is in our relationship
I'm waiting for a Denzel, James Earl James kinda love
that will love me as I begin to graciously grow older
and take me by my hand and lead me down a road full of
beautiful surprises
such as lilies on Friday, Candy on Monday, love
making on Tuesday, loves notes on Wednesday,
bubble baths on Thursday, and bible study's
on Saturdays
I'm waiting for a love that has a backbone and can
stand up to the accusations of the world.
a love that can bring confidence and realism,
As well as finances and hard work to the table
A love that can easily let go of what she did to him
years ago and allow me to be me as I comfort and
bandage up the wounds that have yet to heal
in his heart
I'm waiting for a love that is so deeply rooted in
salvation that he has to go through Jesus just to find me
A love that lives by the word and allows his flesh
to die daily
A love that will have the angels wishing they were
human so that they could feel the love between us
A love that has a language that can only be understood

*by the seraphs that sit at the feet of God in heaven
I'm waiting for a love that leaves me speechless at the
thought of his conversation
and wipes my tears before their even released
from my eyelids
A love that only Nelly and Kelly could sing about
(Cause baby I love you, I need you)
A love that can find me searching for his eyes across the
room as we both think the same thoughts
A love that won't spit poetry to me to drop my panties
but will make love to me verbally
to release my emotions
So if you see him looking as ordinary as me it's okay
for you to speak just let him know I'm seated on the
corner of Patience Avenue wrapped in a blanket of
trust, endurance, and hope*

48
—

Dirty Thirty

Oh, how I wish that was true. I wish I was really in control, but I wasn't. Devin still had a hold over me, and he pulled all the strings of my heart. I wish he didn't mean all those things he said the night of the party, but unfortunately, he did. I know this because a few months later in April, after we had just finished another rendezvous, he told me he was going to ask his girlfriend to marry him.

The Weekend

Is it so bad to give in to temptation to teeter on the edge of lust, fantasy, and ecstasy only to end back at the cove of loneliness and lowered expectations? He said he loved the softness of my lips next to his newly wedded smile, he liked the way my eyes

disappeared as I resented the way I felt next to this
woman's soul mate
I failed miserably at walking away as we made fellatio
our signature kiss
My mind wondered about the countless times he'd
wondered about the color of my lips and how they
would taste in the presence of his kiss
I blushed as we revealed our plans to never let go even
after he'd moved on.
My dimpled smile grew as it ran carelessly across the
ocean of air between us
He asked if I cud keep the secret of our love in the place
that I had secretly held him nearest to (my heart),
There were times I needed to be needed, appreciated,
caressed, and gently touched
But could it actually be genuine?
Or is it just my jewel that he seeks to find uncovered
and moistly kept just for a time as this, when I am in
need of a new breath to touch the sweetness of the nape
of my neck
Pieces of me have come to accept the fact that I will
eventually settle for segments of someone else's heart
That I will take what is dished out for me never
venturing to find fresh food of my own

As you can imagine, I was heartbroken again. And this was yet another pivotal moment in my life in regards to my relationship with food. Between the moment Devin told me he was going to propose and the month of September (about six months), I went from 224 pounds to 254 pounds. Although I had started seeing a psychologist, it still hadn't helped me with my relationship with food.

My therapist was a big help in trying to get me to love me for me. He often pushed me to speak things out as they really were and not as I wanted them to be. Often times, I found myself making excuses for Devin or the men who were previously in my life, when in reality they just were who they were. It didn't matter how much potential they had or how many opportunities I could see in their future. What mattered is where they were at the time we met and how they treated me throughout the relationship we had. My doctor wanted so badly for me to just be honest with myself. I realize now that I just wasn't ready to do that.

Over time, it just became easier to eat my sorrows away than to think about what was going on in my life. Anytime I was stressed or frustrated, my immediate release was food.

I was still that little black, chubby sixth grader who no one liked. So, as usual, I started to let food occupy my time and keep me company when I was alone—which was most of the time. Now don't get me wrong, it's not like I didn't have friends, family or

51

a social life. I had all of those things, but nothing seemed to fill the void of loneliness.

By September, I knew I needed to do something to get my mind off Devin's wedding, so I decided to start going back to the gym and throw myself an awesome 30th birthday bash. Hell, maybe I would even meet someone, and I could finally officially rid myself of the remnants of Devin. Maybe, just maybe, I could meet a guy who would sweep me off my feet and carry me away from the life of a side chick.

I knew I needed to set the perfect atmosphere for a love connection, so I rented out a club in downtown Little Rock and hired a band. I was ready to take over the world and start life anew. I invited every guy that I was even remotely interested in or had even spoken to in the last six months. I decided that whoever showed up was destined to be my new beau.

Well, wouldn't you know it, to my dismay the only guy who showed up was Devin. Yes, this was my life. Always being disappointed is something I had grown accustomed to, but I decided to enjoy my night nevertheless.

That night I wore black, thigh-high boots, black leggings that crisscrossed the outside of my legs and a black and white polka-dotted shirt that had a see through piece that cut right at my cleavage line. I was BAD! And no one could tell me otherwise. There was a roast and toast, and I was able to sit back and enjoy my friends tell HILARIOUS stories about me as the night went

on. I had already decided that toward the end of the show I would grace the stage with a few new pieces, and the time was nearing, when a girlfriend of mine walked in with the exact same dress I had planned on changing into. There was no way that I was going be a twinkie at my birthday party, so I sent my sister, Melissa, to my place to find another outfit.

This was a code red, and it was imperative that I had my party the way I intended it to be. Needless to say, my Melissa made it back in time for me to change clothes and get on stage. She even sang background vocals for me, and we rocked the house. Everyone had a blast!

After performing, various people began to give me hugs and kisses and let me know how much they enjoyed the party. It was at this moment I noticed two guys walk in that I hadn't seen all night. I didn't think much of it until one guy walked up to me and introduced himself. He grabbed my arm and began talking, and honestly, I didn't hear anything he said because all I could see was his masculine shoulders and his dark chocolate skin. I was completely mesmerized. When I finally snapped out of it, I was able to refocus and I politely asked him to repeat everything he had previously stated. He laughed, and I guess chalked it up to the fact that the music was loud and kindly repeated himself. "Hi, I'm Robert, Carol's cousin, we spoke on the phone." I immediately remembered that one of my girlfriends wanted to hook me up with her cousin, and I invited him to come to the party not thinking he would actually do it. Robert then stated, "I

would love to take you out and get to know you better." I'm sure at this point all he could see was my teeth because I was smiling from ear to ear. I got myself together and told him that I'd love to go out with him. He gave me a hug and told me happy birthday and walked away.

This literally made my entire night! I thought to myself, "This is how you do it! Say yes to the first stranger that asks you out! You are in your thirties now, live life, and let live!"

And boy did I live! Robert and I met on September 28 and he moved into my place on November 4. Too quick? Well, that's what happens when the only way you know to get over one guy is to get another guy. Because I moved Robert in, there was now no more room for Devin to pop up and have his way with me.

When I look back now, I know that this was a horrible mistake. I should have been strong enough to end things with Devin and understand that we would never be anything as it relates to a real relationship. Unfortunately, at that time in my life, I wasn't ready to admit that and it was easier for me to yet again just put someone else in Devin's place.

Besides, Robert was great. He was nice, easy going, confident, and more importantly he was mine. Okay, so there were definitely differences between us, but I don't think that people have to be the same person in order to make a relationship work. For example, I had multiple degrees and Robert had his diploma. I grew up in church and Robert grew up in the streets. I'd never smoked weed,

and Robert occasionally did. Either way, it was too late to think about all that now. We were living together and we were happy, so wasn't that all that mattered?

By the time Robert came along, I was back in the gym and working hard to start losing the weight I had gained over the past six months. At this point I was working out every morning and wouldn't be home when Robert finished his night shift. He was so needy and cute. He wanted me to be home when he got home so that he could curl up next to me. So, even though he didn't ask me directly, I started slowly easing up on my morning workouts. I wanted to be next to him as much as he wanted me to be next to him. Our schedules were opposite, so the more time we got while we were both home, the better.

I'm telling you, I couldn't have picked a better stranger to move into my place. I don't think I ever believed in love at first sight but I definitely hit it big when Robert came into my life. Even though we had differences, we made it work. For example, I would make him fried chicken while I ate baked fish. I would make mashed potatoes and macaroni for him while I had a salad. It was definitely a change that was happening in my kitchen, but I could handle making two meals at a time because Robert wasn't really into eating the way I ate. Life was good. I just needed to make a few modifications to accommodate the new love of my life.

So, here it is seven months later and I find out that Robert has a side chick. Who would have thought?

55

I was devastated and gave him an ultimatum after I put him out. It only took him one day to realize how much he missed me and how bad he messed up. We made up and decided we needed to take a mini-vacation and rekindle our love for one another. We moved passed the infidelity and made amends. We decided that all we needed was each other, and that we didn't need any extra people in our relationship.

People make mistakes, and I'm all for forgiving and forgetting. Who was I to say that Robert hadn't changed? I've never been the type of person to hang something over someone's head. I knew I wasn't perfect, and I never expected Robert to be perfect. This was our relationship, and I knew that we could figure it out together.

Life was good.

God said what?

Four months later, after renewing our love and mending our relationship, we moved into a bigger apartment on the nicer side of town.

One morning I needed to use Robert's phone and when I opened it, there was a message waiting for him that said, "Morning baby."

My heart immediately dropped into my stomach, and I immediately started to interrogate him about it. Suddenly, Robert said something that I will never forget and still echoes in my ears from time to time.

"I mean, I'm talking to her but I'm not leaving you."

I was so confused and shocked. I thought we were over this shit. I thought we had decided to be committed to one another and that there wouldn't be other people in our relationship.

Apparently, I was wrong.

I headed towards the door to leave but once I grabbed the handle, I just couldn't leave for some reason. I mean, I literally

couldn't find the strength to leave this man, and I don't know why. I guess I just wasn't strong enough at the time. I went to the other bathroom, stripped down and got into the shower. I stayed there for over 30 minutes. At one point, Robert came in to check on me.

By the time I got out of the shower and got myself together, he was asleep. I found myself waking him up, kneeling down and letting him know that I only wanted to be with him and that I didn't want anyone else interfering in our relationship. In a way, what I really was doing was begging my boyfriend to be faithful to me.

Once again, Robert promised he would be faithful and told me that he loved me. All of this happened three weeks before our one-year anniversary.

At this point, I felt like we needed to be surrounded by people in committed loving relationships. So, what better way to celebrate than to have a dinner?

Since I decided to stay, I knew that it was all or nothing, so I prepared for an anniversary party. I invited a few of my closest friends and a few of his as well. It was a beautiful occasion. I was blessed with a beautiful diamond necklace and I gifted him a watch that had "I love you my king" engraved on the back.

Life was good.

And to celebrate our one-year anniversary, we decided to take a vacation to Los Angeles where we once again rekindled our love for one another. While on vacation, we really just took time to

 More Than

There is more to a relationship than sex.
There is more to a relationship than countless orgasms

enjoy one another. We reminisced about the first time we met, our first kiss, and the first time we expressed our love for one another physically. The vacation went so well that we decided we wanted to spend the rest of our lives vacationing together. Yes, Robert and I decided to get married. And I was as happy as could be.

When we got home, Robert took my parents out for dinner and asked my father for my hand in marriage. It was quite romantic, and I was thrilled to finally be marrying someone who wanted me for me.

Around the same time that we were spreading the good news of the engagement, Robert's car broke down. At this point, I knew that he needed a real car with a warranty and not just some cash car. So as a couple, we made the decision to get him a new vehicle before he purchased my ring. I mean a ring was just a symbol anyway, right?

It took a couple of weeks, but Robert finally found what he wanted, an F-150. He was lit up like a Christmas tree when he took his test drive. I knew this would make him happy, so I co-signed on getting him the truck.

Life was good.

59

09

and multiple sexual explorations of the body.
It's about companionship, trust, and growth.
Companionship is what carries you through hard times
and pushes you to greater heights.
To it, there is no comparison.
In times of loneliness, depression, anguish, pain, and
suffering a penis is not what got me through.
It was companionship with God that kept me from
taking my own life.
It was companionship with friends that got me out of
bed and into a shower.
You see the more you feed your flesh with the lustful
desires of your mind the more you poison your heart.
It then begins to misconceptualize the meaning of love
based on sex.
It begins to taint the mind into thinking that the more
climaxes he gives you the more he loves you.
Companionship will warm you at night when he won't
even answer the phone.
Companionship will keep you sane when he doesn't
even remember your name.
Companionship will bring you soup and wash your
body when sickness leaves you feeble and unable to
dress yourself.

19

Companionship cleans up your puke and wipes your butt when your mind has left you.

Yes sex is a magnificent thing and wonderful to have but in my darkest hours I'd take companionship over a night of passionate kisses and erotic pleasures any day.

62

Not so fast!

So here we are, five months later, after the official announcement of our engagement and we have nine 30-gallon tubs in our second bedroom stuffed with wedding decorations. By this time, we had already won a photographer's package for our wedding and three honeymoons. Things were moving fast and all was well, except in our relationship.

Around this time, Robert had started spending a lot more time with his homeboys and less time with me. Admittedly, I was doing a lot of traveling for work and would often stockpile the fridge with home-cooked meals for him while I was on the road. I thought the traveling would make Robert miss me and want to be home when I returned, but it didn't.

He was changing. There was something different about him, and I couldn't put my finger on why his mood and attitude were starting to change. All I knew was that I wanted things to work

out. I often found myself questioning whether or not I should go through with the wedding, and one day I got the answer to that question.

In mid-April of 2015 (six months until the wedding), I was home alone sitting on the couch waiting for Robert to come home. Suddenly, I heard a voice say, "No". Although I knew I was home alone, I turned and looked around. I tried to shake it off, but again I heard the voice say, "No". I started talking to God and said, "Surely you're not telling me not to marry this guy? I have wedding stuff in the next room." I got such a quickening in my spirit, and I knew that it was God telling me not to get married.

As much as it was going to hurt to have that conversation, I knew that it had to be done. I knew I had to be obedient to what I knew God was telling me.

Later that day when Robert came home, I broke the news to him. I let him know that I didn't think we would be ready for marriage in six months and that we needed more time. As you can imagine, he was furious and the next few weeks became unbearable to say the least. Robert really wanted to marry me and was embarrassed to tell the family that we were postponing the wedding.

Although I let Robert know that I wanted to continue to work on our relationship, that didn't mean much to him. The distance between us began to grow more and more. Once again, I began to turn to food to cope with what was going on. I also made the

decision to start searching for a place of my own. Maybe things would get better if we had some space.

Little did I know that I would be moving out sooner than later. One day Robert and I had to switch vehicles so that I could transport some furniture. When I finally got home on May 21, 2015, Robert was exhausted from what apparently had been a hard day. I kissed him and headed to my truck to give him some peace and quiet at home alone. To my dismay, when I got in my truck I found seeds of weed sprinkled on my drivers stick and in my coin tray.

As you can imagine, I was livid. I collected the seeds and stormed back into the apartment, waking up Robert. The first thing I did was to ask a dumb question, "Baby, have you been smoking weed in my truck?" Robert's response was, "No, what the hell are you talking about?" By this point, my lucidity had gone to an undefined level. I placed the weed seeds in his hand as proof (as if he didn't know what he had done).

At that moment, Robert called me a liar and stormed out of the house upset at the fact that I had broken his sleep.

Whelp, ladies and gentlemen, this was the "I've had it moment." Upon his exit, I called my old landlord and asked if he had a place that I could move into immediately. At this point, it was 1:15 p.m. Once my landlord let me know that I could come and pick up the keys to my new place at 2:15, I didn't hesitate on making the next phone call.

I called my girls.

We all know who the girls are right? That one set of friends that are ready to do anything you need done in the case of an emergency. Well, if you don't have a group of girls, I strongly suggest you get some. I picked up the keys to my apartment at 2:15, and I was completely moved out of our apartment and hanging up photos in my new place at 6:37 p.m.

Love or Lust?

The next day, apparently, Robert returned home to find an empty house. He was amazed that I left him. And I assured him that I would not be returning.

Four weeks into being single, the loneliness began to kick in. Robert had finally apologized himself back into my heart and into my bed. I thought maybe this was exactly what we needed. Maybe we just needed to start over and live in separate places. Maybe life could be good again.

Who was I fooling? It wasn't even a full three months later when my honey was laying in my bed asleep after we had had sex and I fed him breakfast that I received an unexpected phone call from my sister-in-law. She wasn't really making much sense and I didn't want to make a lot of noise while Robert was asleep, so I told her I'd call her later.

I decided to take a drive to clear my head. I felt like my relationship

was in shambles and that I was holding on to something that deep down inside I knew I needed to let go. Honestly, I knew that this relationship was not the plan God had for my life. As I drove around the city, I began to ask myself, "How can I be in a relationship with someone that I don't trust." Suddenly, God clearly said to me that it was impossible.

Even with knowing that God was right and that He clearly wanted more for me, I didn't know if I was ready to let Robert go yet.

Two hours later, I found myself working on some edits for a friend's resume when my phone rang (at approximately 11:17 a.m., August 26). This time it was my sister and she had my sister-n-law on the phone as well. Seemingly, earlier that morning when my sister-n-law called me, what she was trying to tell me was that she had seen Robert with another woman. How crazy is it that the errand Robert needed to run while using my truck was actually him taking this woman to work? And since he didn't have much gas, he needed to use my vehicle. When my sister-in-law saw him pull up at her job, she thought it was me and Robert, then she quickly realized it was another woman. I thanked my sister-in-law for letting me know this unfortunate news and hung up the phone.

Now, I am sure that some of you may have been thinking that it was time for me to wake him up with a skillet across his head, slash his tires, punch him, slap him, or something in that realm. However, that's not how I roll.

Instead, I went into my bedroom and gently woke up Robert. "Baby, baby, you need to wake up. I just got a call that you had someone else in my truck and you have to get out of here." Of course, he woke up confused and "caught." I told him he needed to get his clothes on and gather his things and leave my home. Robert slowly got himself together and came into the living room where I was continuing to edit the resume and asked me, "So, what do we do now?" I just looked at him and said, "I don't know, but you need to leave."

I shed a few tears in front of him and let him know that I had given him so much of my life and I just didn't understand why that wasn't enough.

Robert left my home and I calmed my nerves and completed the edit on my friend's resume. I was not going to let yet another unfortunate event ruin my day or my life.

Three hours later, Robert called me to ask for gas money so he could get to work. And this was the moment that I lost it. I screamed to the top of my lungs and told him that I had no money and that the only thing I had left to give him was blood. In return, Robert stated that whoever saw him was mistaken and that it wasn't him. He was so angry that I didn't believe him, that he broke up with me.

The irony.

As you can imagine, the next few months were hard. Robert would call or text in an effort to see if we could work things out,

but I refused. I was truly done this time.

Unfortunately for me, he was not. He was bitter and wanted to get back at me for leaving him. And that truly is what he did.

"I sat back and I thought to myself, what is it that she loves, how can I hurt her? And then it came to me, you love your credit. Since you don't want to be with me, I'll ruin your credit." This is what Robert said to me after having missed two payments on the truck and letting the insurance lapse. I couldn't believe that after being finally free from the relationship that I was still connected to him in such a way that it was impacting my financial freedom.

I let Robert know that although I was not a fighter physically, I was a fighter mentally. I told him that if he didn't do right by me that I would take him to court.

I can remember wanting to be a lawyer when I was in the third grade. Little did I know that over 20 years later, I'd be representing myself in a civil court case.

It was time to prove to myself that I wasn't as weak as I thought I was. I was an intelligent woman who made the mistake of tying myself to someone unworthy of me.

It was past time for being upset. I needed to take action. So, I headed to the law library and starting researching how I could take Robert to court and get possession of the truck back.

If there ever is a moment in your life where you feel like you don't have power over what is going on in your life, pray. Over

the next 11 months, I prayed over my situation and believed God would deliver a victory in my life. I had been too long separated from Him, and I came back with my arms open and in need of a miracle. God truly showed up and showed out in my life throughout that duration of time. I met several people that helped me in different ways. Although the process was long, it was worth it and it showed me that with God, persistence and determination, I could complete any task set before me.

I represented myself in court and won my case plus a garnishment against Robert. The day of my final court date, the judge turned off the microphone and said, "Congratulations," and as I walked out of the courtroom, the bailiff whispered "You won, congratulations."

Tears fell from my eyes as I exited the courthouse. All I could think was, I did it! I did it! God, we did it! I just cried all the way to my car. Although I knew it wasn't over yet, I had done everything legally in my power to amend the situation.

Three days later, I was back at the courthouse filing a motion against Robert for contempt of court. At this time, he wasn't even driving the truck but he still didn't want to give up its location.

Needless to say, once he realized that contempt of court meant possibly jail time, he gave up the location of the vehicle, and I was able to turn it back over to the bank.

It was finally over.

I was free.

Or so I thought.

Live and Let Love

So here I am, living free.

By this time, I had ballooned up to 319. I was working from home full of stress, depressed, angry and relieved all at the same time. And I was single.

What was I to do?

Basically, my entire life I had been looking for someone to love me for me. I had been looking for someone to validate my beauty. And I had been looking for someone to want me.

The reality of it all was that I first needed to do all those things for myself. How was I ever going to love someone or expect someone to love me when I didn't even know myself? It just wasn't possible.

I decided to start my weight loss journey and commit to losing 100 pounds over the next two years. I wanted to take a journey with myself and discover who Jessica really was deep down

inside. I knew that it wasn't going to be easy but I knew it would be necessary. The scariest thing about the entire journey was dealing with my reflection. Not the reflection that showed how large I had gotten over time, but the reflection that showed I was so deeply wounded.

I loved so hard and so much, till that love was used against me. Each of us are raised in different environments and those environments are what shape us into the adults that we become. I was born and raised in the Church of God in Christ, and I was saved and filled with the Holy Ghost at the age of 11. I was speaking in tongues by the age of 16. Meanwhile, Robert didn't know what a "helpmate" was. What did I really expect from this relationship? Why was I so ready to be someone's girlfriend that I settled for the first someone willing to hand me that title?

Where was I in my life that I couldn't find the love and admiration I needed within the arms of God? Where was I in my faith that I was willing to give up the common-sense things for the right-now things? Where was Jessica? Sometimes you have to ask yourself, am I here? Am I present? Am I presenting the best me that I can be to myself? Not the best me for everyone else, but is this the best me for me? Am I giving all I have to give to Jessica? Or have I given every ounce of myself to someone that doesn't even know how to love the way I love? Have I given myself to someone who isn't willing to learn the way I love?

I want not only to be converted by the blood. I want to be covered by the love of a man that knows Jesus Christ as his

personal savior. I forgot that along the way. I got so caught up in the physical and in the day-to-day motions of life that I became robotic and dead to the pain of what I was feeling inside, emptiness. I was alone while lying next to a beautifully built man who had the entire physical package but was as empty as a shell inside with nothing to offer me.

As I look back, I can remember saying to Robert, "I love you, I know you're a hustler and a liar, but I love you and you don't have to be anyone else other than your true self when it comes to me."

I was so accepting and so honest with a man that wasn't even able to comprehend who I was as a woman. Not just any woman, but a woman of God. But how could he even see a woman of God? I wasn't going to church regularly, I wasn't reading my bible regularly. I was just living.

Sometimes we think we are lifting people up to our wonderful level of greatness when in reality they have already taken us down to their level.

Looking at my reflection was so hard in the beginning. It's amazing how hard it is to do something that seems so simple. But when you spend the last two years of your life taking care of a man and not taking care of yourself, when the time comes to face yourself in the mirror, you do not really want to deal with what you see and that is where I found myself. In tears, afraid to start living again.

So, what do I do? I went from being in a place where I thought

75

I knew who I was, to a place where I was lost and not sure if I would ever be found again. When I met Robert, I was trying to escape Devin and I was 254 pounds. It was no one else's fault but my own and no one was going to be able to get the weight off except for me.

So, I decided to take my life back. I decided to do whatever it took to get me to the place where I knew I needed to be, healthy. Healthy would not only be in the physical but spiritually, mentally and physically as well.

At this point, I'd been a member of 10 Fitness membership for over seven months and decided to actually start using it. I started going to the gym every day and being more mindful of what I was eating.

I started experiencing food. Really experiencing it. I became more about taste and flavors rather than consumption. I tried new recipes, some I liked and some I didn't. I started chewing my food 22 times. I started tasting food for the first time. I decided to discover what I truly liked to eat, just like Julia Roberts in *Runaway Bride*. I didn't even know what type of eggs I liked.

I like my eggs over medium or poached. Who would have thought it?

Most importantly and above everything else, I started praying more. I started falling to my knees and asking God to help me fight my food addiction. Yes, I had a food addiction. It had been

76

I had to face the fact that I had food issues. I began to pray sincerely before each meal and asked God to help me not to over indulge. Sometimes I would find myself crying because the spirit of depression or loneliness would try and overtake me, and in return I would want to eat. I had to pray and ask God to help me. The prayers came from a deep, deep, dark place of what I felt like was unworthiness. Did I really deserve to lose weight, because I would just get depressed and gain the weight again? Did I really need to understand who I was because I would meet someone and lose who I was all over again?

I prayed for guidance, and thankfully God gave it to me and let me know that I was not alone and that even in something as small as portion control, He would be with me. He helped me to understand that as much as I had decided to love other people that He loved me all the more. As much as I ran from Him and into the arms of false lovers, He still wanted me to be happy and to thrive in life.

God helped me to become a better me.

Over time, I also realized that I couldn't lose the weight by myself. Although God was keeping my mind on the course I had set before me, I needed some additional help in the flesh.

It didn't take long for me to realize that I needed to return to Kameelah at WOW Fitness.

By the time I returned to her, I had lost about 15 pounds. I must admit I was embarrassed to go back to her having been 224 since the last time I had weighed in. Kameelah was welcoming and let me know she would be right there with me while I worked my way back to health.

I must say that it wasn't only Kameelah, but it was the women that attended the gym as well. Each of them had their own goals but each was willing to cheer one another on. This truly was a place for me to flourish and to grow in love.

This time around, I decided to try my luck at something I had never done before, Zumba.

It was hard in the beginning. I didn't know how to control my breath, and I didn't have the endurance to make it through the songs that came back to back. It really felt like it was never ending, LOL. Needless to say, I decided to not give up and to give it all I had.

Over the next year, I lost about 50 pounds.

January 2016	319.0 lbs.
February	314.0 lbs.
March	309.2 lbs.
April	304.0 lbs.

May	296.8 lbs.
June	294.4 lbs.
July	277.4 lbs.
August	268.4 lbs.
September	268.0 lbs.
October	262.0 lbs.
November	264.0 lbs.
December	266.0 lbs.
January 2017	268.0 lbs.

Between January and June, I fluctuated between 264 and 273. During this time, I didn't "diet." I simply ate and drank whatever I wanted to and continued to do Zumba. Once June came, I decided I had "maintained" enough and was ready to start losing weight again. I knew that I wanted to lose 100 pounds and the target date I set for myself was approaching fast. A part of why I maintained that same weight was to answer a question many people would ask me: "Once you lose the weight, how do you maintain it?"

For me, the answer was simple. "Never stop working out and continue to enjoy food without overindulging."

I know it seems easier said than done. That's because it is. I'm not telling you that I have all the answers and that it was easy or is easy for me to look over "good" food. But I am telling you that

once I made my mind up and decided I wanted something better for my life, that was all it took. For me, weight loss is a battle of the mind and willpower.

And please understand that I eat fried chicken, French fries, lasagna, pizza, burgers, etc. BUT…I eat all of that in moderation. I no longer eat myself into an "it is" frenzy. What's "it is," you ask? It is how people feel after they have had a really "good" meal. In reality, it's probably more related to eating processed foods that contain high levels of sugar and refined carbohydrates. Foods like this causes a rise in blood sugar levels, followed by a drop, which results in low energy levels, also known as the "it is."

Take time to examine how you feel after you eat. Food is supposed to be energy and fuel the body. If you are feeling sleepy and sluggish after a meal, you may need to examine what type of food you are allowing into your temple.

Now here it is July of 2017, and I am back to the grind of working out and eating to actually lose weight because—please know—that there is a difference in eating just to eat and actually eating foods that will help you lose weight.

Since I had been doing Zumba (cardio) in the evenings, I realized that I wasn't lifting any weights or doing as much toning as I felt I needed. So, I decided to take the advice of a friend and start attending a 6 a.m. boot camp held Monday through Thursday. YES! That means that I would be working out Monday through Thursday from 6 to 7 a.m. and 5:30 p.m. to 7 p.m. I know this

may seem extreme to some, but for me it wasn't. It was just the extra boost I needed to ensure I would meet my weight loss goals.

Even with the extra workout, I still felt like I was missing something. I had gone through so much, and I felt like there were other people in the world just like me. I felt like there were men and women who were struggling with their weight and didn't have a support system. So, I decided to start a weight loss company called Budda Inspired (B Inspired).

My hope is that it will become a movement fueled by change. I want to change the minds of people and what they think weight loss means.

To me, weight loss starts in the mind and transfers to the body. B Inspired is about discovering the goals you have deep down inside and asking yourself what keeps you from reaching those goals.

During my journey, I had to decide I wanted my life to be about more than pizza, chicken spaghetti, ice cream and cookies. I had to make the conscious decision to live beyond the meals that I enjoyed.

I had to decide to live beyond breakfast, lunch and dinner. I had to decide to live past the broken relationships and the broken promises.

I had to decide to live.

Nowadays, I literally eat to live, NOT live to eat. This means I am

aware of the food that I am putting into my body and the effects it will have on my temple. As much as I love potatoes, I now finally understand that the more potatoes (of any kind) I eat, the less likely it is that I will lose weight.

So, do I still eat potatoes? Of course, I do. I simply eat them in moderation and I chose the right time of day and day of the week to have those potatoes. If I know I'll be having anything of high-calorie substance during the week, I will more than likely eat it on a day that I will have two workouts. This will enable me to burn off more of those calories.

I'm not a mathematician, and I don't spend time weighing food and calculating calories, but I do use common sense. It is better to eat French fries on a Monday if I'll have two intense workouts than on a Friday when I know I'm only going to moderately walk two miles.

B Inspired was birthed through my own transgressions and hardships. This platform has allowed me to reach people in different areas and in different stages of their life. Most importantly, B Inspired has allowed me to be transparent and share my story freely and unashamed.

Before each one of my meals I pray and ask God for strength to get through the meal without over indulging. Because I know my weakness and my struggles I'm okay with turning something as simple as food over to God. Where I am weak He will always be strong for me.

If you learned nothing from reading my story, I pray you learned that you don't have to live life in the shadows of your old self. You don't have to be a slave to the food you eat. You don't have to be afraid to walk into a gym because of your size. You don't have to be afraid to be yourself.

Take the time to love and hug on yourself and daily remind yourself that you are beautiful. The same way my mother did it to me, you can do it for yourself.

Look in that mirror and state the beautiful things about your features. Don't point out what you don't like. Take the time to love on yourself and start your journey today.

Don't be held captive to food because of your emotions. Don't blame your job, the kids or your busy life for the unhealthy things you allow into your temple. Take your life back!

Please know that it's not too late to start seeing a psychologist about the things that happened to you in your past. It's not too late to share your past hurts with your parents or loved ones. It's not too late to start putting yourself first above other people's needs.

The time has come for you to take care of yourself and for you to love yourself enough to get healthy and stay healthy.

Over the past two years, I didn't let anyone discourage me from working out. I didn't talk myself out of eating better. I simply took it one meal at a time and one workout at a time. That is and will forever be my motto.

Past Life

As I look back over pictures and shed tears over past decisions and bad mistakes I realize that's all they are...past...there's no need to continue to relive that moment over and over again. I am not who I once was and that's okay. I don't look the same as I looked yesterday and my life has changed even in these few moments. I press on for I know today will be better than yesterday and tomorrow may not come but my present is here in this place right now......

I may not be where I want to be, but I am definitely not where I once was. Though I've had heartaches and headaches, I've finally found Jessica again. I know who she is and I know what she needs to be happy. I know that it is of the utmost importance that I never allow myself to give away something as precious as my virtue and my time to someone who is not worthy of it. That worthiness stems from the value I place on my own life. And I now know that my life is worth more than a kiss, a donut, a cookie, or a burger. I am worth more than any midnight snack, and I will be forever grateful to God for helping me finally realize that.

Made in the USA
Columbia, SC
11 February 2018

Made in the USA
Charleston, SC
01 October 2013

Working the Wreckage of the American Poem
   edited by RD Armstrong (2011)
Living Among the Mangled (revised)
   by RD Armstrong, special edition, (2011)
The Accidental Navigator by Henry Denander (2011)
Catalina by Laurie Soriano (2011)* SPD
Born to Be Blue by Tony Moffeit (2011)
Last Call: the Bukowski Legacy Continues
   edited by RD Armstrong (2011)
Strong As Silk by Brigit Truex (2012)* SPD
The Instrument of Others by Leonard J. Cirino (2012)
If It We by Lisa Zaran (2012)*
The Names of Lost Things by Jason Hardung (2012)
Because, Just Because by Philip Ramp (2012)
Crazy Bone by Billy Jones (2012)
LUMMOX Magazine edited by RD Armstrong
   (see description below)(2012)
5150—A Memoir by Dana Christensen (2013)*
I See Hunger's Children by normal (2013)*
her by j/j hastain (2013)*

   LUMMOX (the magazine) returned in November of 2012 as a yearly print magazine. It contains interviews, essays, articles, reviews, artwork, ads and lots of poetry (future issues will also feature special flashbacks to the old *LUMMOX Journal* archives). The focus of the first issue was "Favorite Poems," the theme for #2 is PLACE. Each issue features poetry from around the world, and is presented, in part, by "Guest Editors" (poets themselves) who will highlight 8-10 of their favorite poets, with 1-2 poems each.

   LUMMOX will be available by annual subscription for $25 USA and $35 WORLD; it will also be listed on Amazon for $30 + shipping. Visit *www.lummoxpress.com/journal.html* for details.

The following books are available directly from the LUMMOX Press via its website: *www.lummoxpress.com* or at LUMMOX c/o PO Box 5301, San Pedro, CA 90733. There are also E-Copy (PDF) versions of most titles available. Books with the letters SPD are also carried by Small Press Distribution.

The Wren Notebook by Rick Smith (2000)
Last Call: The Legacy of Charles Bukowski
  edited by RD Armstrong (2004)
On/Off the Beaten Path by RD Armstrong (2008)
Fire and Rain—Selected Poems 1993-2007, Volumes 1 & 2 by RD Armstrong (2008)*
El Pagano and Other Twisted Tales
  by RD Armstrong (short stories – 2008)*
New and Selected Poems by John Yamrus (2009)
The Riddle of the Wooden Gun by Todd Moore (2009)
Sea Trails by Pris Campbell (2009)
Down This Crooked Road—Modern Poetry from the Road Less Traveled edited by RD Armstrong and William Taylor, Jr. (2009)
Drive By by John Bennett (2010)
Modest Aspirations by Gerald Locklin & Beth Wilson (2010)
Steel Valley by Michael Adams (2010)*
Hard Landing by Rick Smith (2010)
A Love Letter to Darwin by Jane Crown (2010)*
E/OR—Living Amongst the Mangled
  by RD Armstrong (2010)
Ginger, Lily & Sweet Fire by H. Lamar Thomas (2010)*
Whose Cries Are Not Music by Linda Benninghoff (2011)*
Dog Whistle Politics by Michael Paul (2011)*
What Looks Like an Elephant by Edward Nudleman (2011)* SPD

ABOUT THE LUMMOX PRESS

LUMMOX Press was created in 1994 by **RD Armstrong**. It began as a self-publishing/DIY imprint for poetry by RD, aka Raindog. Several chapbooks were published and in late 1995 LUMMOX began publishing *The LUMMOX Journal*, a monthly small/underground press lit-arts mag. Available primarily by subscription, the *LJ* continued its exploration of the "creative process" until its demise as a print mag in 2006. It was hailed as one of the best monthlies in the small press by John Berbrich and Todd Moore.

In 1998, LUMMOX began publishing the Little Red Book series, and continues to do so, sporadically, today. To date there are some 60 titles in the series and a collection of poems from the first decade of the series has been published under the title, **The Long Way Home** (2009); it's a great way to explore the series.

Together with Chris Yeseta (Layout and Art Direction since 1997), RD continues to publish books that are both striking in their looks as well as their content...*published because of the merit of the work, not the fame of the author.* That's why there are so many first full-length collections in the roster (look for the *).

Some other books and chapbooks by D.R. Wagner include:

97 POEMS
Private Archeology
Pentecost
Horses At The Edge of The Sea
A Limited Means of Expression
Where The Stars Are Kept
Cruisin' At The Limit
The Dimensions of the Morning
Round, Earth, Poems.
The Lost Carnival & Other Poems
The Union Camp Papers
The Day is a Prayer They Can't Understand
   (letters to d.a. levy)
The Egyptian Stroboscope (with d.a. levy)
April 15, April 16
Book for Barb
Four Dreams of Leaves and Dreamers of the Land
Putah Creek Overflow
Sprounds & Vigibles
Defining Zero Spaceform From A Chair Swing
100 Aspects of the Moon
All The Broken Toys in Heaven

internationally and are included in numerous publications and museum collections. He is, further, a professional musician, working as a singer-songwriter and playing guitar and keyboards. He has taught Design at the University of California at Davis since 1988. He also teaches in the Honors program at the University conducting classes in Poetry by Design. His most recent books include a collection of his poetry and photographs tapestries for Rattlesnake Press, entitled Where The Stars Are Kept. In 2011 Rattlesnake Press published a new collection of poetry entitled A Limited Means of Expression. They also reprinted a poetry chapbook of his from 1968 originally published by Black Rabbit Press, Cleveland, Ohio called THE DIMENSIONS OF THE MORNING. A new chapbook PENTECOST, has been published by Green Panda Press , Cleveland, Ohio 2012 and his book PERSONAL ARCHEOLOGY will premiere this year from Bottle of Smoke Press, Dover, DE. Most recently his book 97 POEMS was published by Cold River Press, Grass Valley, CA. He continues to design interior carpeting and tapestry as well as write, perform and publish poetry regularly. He currently lives in Elk Grove, Ca.

D.R. Wagner is the author of over twenty books and chapbooks of poetry and letters. He founded press : today : niagara and Runcible Spoon (press) in the late 1960s and produced over fifty magazines and chapbooks. He co-wrote The Egyptian Stroboscope with d.a. levy in the late 1960s. His work is much published and has appeared in many translations. He is also a visual artist, producing miniature needle-made tapestries that have been exhibited

Acknowledgements

There are so many people to thank for helping me get through this book. I will make a short list but if you are not here, it is only because my mind abandons me on occasion and I later find myself distressed that I have not included you in this list. Please consider yourself included.

From the past: Kenneth Patchen, d.a. levy, Jorge Luis Borges, Eduardo Carrillo.

Now: E.R. Baxter III, Bill Yates, T.L. Kryss, Michael McClure, Douglas Blazek, H. Brown Miller, Ann Menebroker, Viola Weinberg, Todd Walton, Kirk Robertson, Jan Jett, Ryan Jett, Patrick Grizzell, Jane Blue, Ed Sanders, Meg Pokrass, Alice Anderson, Leslie Haber, Michael Madden, Even and Eve Myquest, Andy Jones, Kieth Ball, Taylor Graham, Katy Thomas, John Dorsey, James Jobe, Bari Kennedy, Robert Lee Haycock, Kathy Kieth, Sean Harold, Patrick Q. Minor, Tom and Desa Bushnell, Al Winans, Michael Robert Pollard for his fine cover and my photograph of his sculpture he gave me long ago, my family, all of them, my Lisa, Dave Boles, Kent Taylor, the poets of Cleveland past and present, the Design Department and its students at UC Davis, and of course R.D. Armstrong and LUMMOX Press for believing in this book.

D.R. Wagner

LOOKING AT THE LIFE OF A FRIEND

Not where one would expect to find
Anything, let alone deep feelings.
The streets seemed too full of people.
The countryside was hurt and much too old.

When we stood on the edge of the road
The landscape seemed to shake as if
It were nervous that we should be there.
Our arms hung at our sides, knives drawn.

We really didn't want any of this.
We were tired of the constant drum of words
In our ears, our inability to make sense
Wherever they were concerned.

We wanted them gone. Perhaps then
We could have a good look at him,
The place he finally decided to confront us
After all the traveling, the tracking,
The hope that we would see him
Directly before us like a sign

Where his life streamed out behind
Him in a clattering of moments tossed
One upon the other, not even trying
To make sense of each other's presence.

CHIME
...for William Blake

I was unwound. I speak in tongues.
The deep trains begin their low
Distant chanting far away, oh so far away.

My sister enters covered with flocks of birds.
They are brilliantly colored
And do not harm her. They
Are her songs. They carry her
Voice high into the heavens.

We slide into a vortex unable to determine
Surfaces of the ocean from its depths.

Angels of light transform us.
We try to laugh but it is impossible.

We are feeling too much at one time.
Even as we walk the streets
Thousands of things are being born.
They will transform the world
Before we reach the parks.

All around us they begin to eat
The animals as quickly
As they are able. It is never
Enough. Gunfire begins.

'Proceed in an orderly fashion to the exits.'
The fire trucks are heard coming closer.

Someone picks up a guitar.
Someone else a drum.
We begin to make music, to sing.
We hope the song never stops. We promise
We will never be asleep again.

D.R. Wagner

STEPS

We can hear the bridge coming
Down as we leave the village.
It is night, God, is it ever night.
The moon hiding just beyond the hills,
Half dressed and frightened looking,
For all its shadow making light.

We can hear the great stones crashing
Into the river, first slowly then
Quickening and insistent.

We're not coming back this way again.
The horses begin to paw the ground,
Shake their heads and shiver in the air.
We will take the horses and leave
As quickly as we can do so.

The smell of death is everywhere.

We didn't cause the war.
We can't help it if we need to eat,
If we need to live and the women
Were so lovely even as they huddled
Into the corners of their ruined buildings.

"Thou shalt not kill." someone says
Almost under their breath.
Listen to the very power of the words.

CRUCIBLE

From here it looked very much
Like a cartoon. All the movements
Were kind of jerky and forced.

As we drew closer we could see
The huge flocks of birds wheeling
And swirling in many colors.

It was beautiful and noisy with
Thousands of bird voices filling
The air and the gray rain just
Starting to fall making them glisten
Even more.

When we drew close upon them we
Could see they were circling above
A city filled with dead human beings.

The streets heaped with silence.
The stench overpowering. We had
To lead our animals away from the
Place quickly. The birds still above
In their mad flight, around and around.

This could be anywhere we recalled
That evening as we gained high ground.
There was no indication of any conflict
Just the crucible of the dead littered
Like driftwood and as black.

We stared into the fire a long time.
Then someone began to sing softly.
Before too long we were all singing.
It was a song without words and a
Million melodies all at once. Somehow
It was soothing. We began to return
To our bodies like angels descending.

D.R. Wagner

MISUNDERSTANDING

Somehow it got into my mind
That you meant something completely
Different than I had supposed you did.

Funny how that works. I don't suppose
It happens all by itself. "Summer
Is a long way off now. I can't remember
What the flowers looked like."

We were staying at that hotel
Near the shore we liked so much.
The air was a curious color of
Red-violet and when we spoke
We knew what we were saying.
Love, that was the stuff. Parts
Of dreams caught in the trees,
Shaking themselves furiously
To get free of their meaning.

I dressed slowly and kept looking
Over at you. Your shoulders, your
Fine hands, the way you gazed out
The windows toward that golden light.

There were many small fires that night
All along the beaches. They were so beautiful.
And your lips. your lips.

AN ANCIENT BATTLE

The battle had long been forgotten.
Someone found a coin recently that had
An image of a sword and a nearly
Obliterated date that someone else
Said was a reference to a particular
Battle. Everyone had died who could
Carry the name of the conflict into
The present. There were layers upon
Layers of dreams that could no
Longer be cut through. Not even
The sound of cloth tearing. no reasons
At all except maybe a hawk announcing
A field to whomever might be interested.

I fell to my knees and prayed for those
Who had been this battle, not even
Certain I could pronounce the place
Correctly. The dream rustled and
Tried to weave my sleep with its images
Of horses terrified and the loud noises
The dying made. Within a week the
Coin had become lost again.
The hawk long disappeared.

D.R. Wagner

Cities, I see you there, copper
Glistening in the copper dawn
Light, crackling in the copper
Colored air, boiling water in
Huge copper pots, pliable
And bending, easily shaped
Like our own dear souls, stolen,
Melted and reformed into useful implements.

So often we forget our own society
And see it become other than this ore
As we tread the copper tinged waves
Forever drawing us closer to that
Blue breath poured against our
Bodies as we conduct all that copper
Into a way of saying we shall ever understand.

COPPER

It's the copper sulfate that turns
The hydrangeas that blue of oxygen
Exhausted blood, making these full
Flowers beacons to bees foraging,
That we may know sweetness
From all the earth.

The verdigris on my hands
Has been rubbed from the copper
Pipes I have been twisting together so
We can have water on the upper
Stories of the house. I can
Feel the water moving through the pipes.
It is mumbling about a blue
Green language infecting
Everything it comes
In contact with.

In my grandfather's room stacks
Of old pennies are piled against the walls
Filling the space with the scent
Of copper coins. Coins with dates
Stamped onto them recalling
All of his life for him. There were
Indian heads and Lincoln portraits.

There is precious little that is
Worth remembering about the
Electric lines high up the towers
Where hawks and hot stick linemen
Command the hum of energy
Through the great body of air.

D.R. Wagner

LIPS PRESSED TOGETHER

There is a shining here that sounds
To me like something should be done.
It reaches out its hand and it is shining
And it is touching itself like fire in the veins
And no one has its name and no one has its number.

Photographs of children who need food
Walk out of magazines and populate
The earth. And there is still the sound
And it is like the hand of God shaking
A small burn to cool itself. And it wears
The face of my own brother.

Finally, as though it really could find a place to end
The last of the birds settle toward a tree
And we reach around it. It is May again. The
Sun becomes its own light, and sound shines
Through all of us, by our kind
Moving in the wind. We call this the making of love
To one and another. Something that is seldom done.

NOTHING VANISHES

These pools look as if the season
Has forgotten them, left them to struggling
As their dark tadpoles struggle, barely able
To cover themselves with what water remains,
Tiny, amphibian feet pushing the mud aside.

They leave no track when they dry. The cracked
earth, the clicking of cicadas upon the best of summer.
A puff of dust pulled up from skeleton bird nests,
Finger bone left by a wind that was not supposed
To have a skeleton. It was supposed to disappear
Into the woods, only dogs would be able to track
It. But for the fires and the cold light of the stars
We would not know of this at all, thinking that
The season had fallen exactly there and the
Change to Autumn would feel like someone
Had only slipped a ring on our finger and we
Would not notice it until the temperatures dropped.

Until it was October all around us once again,
A few rain storms causing the pools to appear
Again. A willow tree insisting it knew what desire
Was all about, urging us on deeper and deeper,
Across the meadows, into the darker woods.

'This all looks so familiar' we would think,
But we would have been changed by everything
We had seen, sit on a fallen tree trunk, listening
Carefully to the croaking of the frogs.

D.R. Wagner

RADIO

The skies realize no one
Can ever stop them. They fashion
Instruments out of birds and ask the wind
To play upon them. If not
The wind something equally
Sightless and brooding
With moods that could make
A child weep.

The page never gives up color
By itself. It remains white,
Looked over and guarded by sharp
Teeth always making up its own story.

The waves are changing again.
The long speeches are coming to an end.
The rationalizations begin looking
For a way to convince our selves that
We knew this was coming all along.
I've described the scene this way so you

Might see that beautiful girl loaded with
Bright colors walking right through
The center of this whole thing
Singing, quite content with how it turned out.

X

D.R. Wagner

When all is accomplished
We too will be transfigured.
You will see the purity of our intentions
And hail us as true instruments
Of conscious news unleashed on the most
trying of times, not content with the ordinary
And willing to auction
Everything you have read
For the warm jets truth
Will bring to our visions.

I will bring you a cloak made of days.
All their weather and possibilities.
It will be our church.
Pray for us.

Breaking and Entering

My thoughts are surprised
To find they have become
Crows overnight and leave
In dark flocks squawking
Loudly, confused at what once
Was a lovely pastoral
Landscape, searching for food.

We've come to take you home,
Rife with the cast off
Carapaces of ten thousand
Prophecies, the husks of as many
Songs, the fragile wings of dragonflies

And persistent banging
Against the doors of heaven.
Clouds of black mosquitos
Sizzle around us,
A music filled with
Borrowed blood built
On the edge of a perfection
Of chance and persistent hope
Huddled together in curious embrace.

Leave us now.
We are no longer afraid.
The way is crisp with moonlight.
The dogs are anxious for the hunt.
Taste has made our mouths unreasonable.
We will cross the mountains.
We understand the promises.
We accept this way of communicating.

D.R. Wagner

BUILDING

Open your mouth. I will open my mouth.
There will be words. They will play
Upon the teeth and thread themselves
Into the splendor that was our
Living body, our hearts so in love, our gaze.
The objects hardest to break remain.

We keep waiting for the gaze to come.
It has traveled a long way now
And finds solace in the scent of cinnamon,
Any gestures that sparkle like gems
As they unravel and become fragments.

*

I broke the front
while going up
and what
came before
was thorn
on cheek
from across
the bay
to pull a tear
from both my eyes

Breaking and Entering

And singing. Singing. And I am
Singing and I was wearing that same
Clothing the morning wears when
It has something to show to us
That is beyond compare and we
Know it. We wish to repeat
It each time we wear these things.

Having coffee near the dooryard
The moss-covered skull so green,
So beautiful, holding the whitest
Pearl in its teeth like the truth.

We can walk here once again. Messages
From flights of geese sent to the seasons.
We climb the little hill just near
The dingle and recognize everything.
So perfect is the singing we are
Able to invent new words against it.

D.R. Wagner

THE CLOTHING OF THE MORNING

The room seems very tiny
As if it could not contain
such a deep sorrow so easily.

The hole extends through the floor
With drifts of dull colored lights
Waiting around the edges of the sore.

We can't wait any longer. We have
Seen the loved ones taken away
Into the night and have chased
After them as far as this room.

We will find a way to enter the room.
We have already begun to learn
The speech of the guardians at the doors.

One of them asked if we have keys,
Another if we knew where the drinking
Liquid was kept. We told them yes
And led them to the desert edge.

Three of us entered the room
At that time. We could hear
The weeping. We must trust
That everyone is telling the truth.

CEREMONY

So many voices. A chorus
Speaking together. There is
Grace in the way the words
Form here. We have no idea
What is being said. But there

It is, pure and outlandish
As late June with its
Dreams of water and Summer
Love caught in its loins.

We walk along the sidewalks
On the edges of the park.
The fireflies are just starting
To be seen so we sit and wait
For the dark to consume everything.

I am in love with you, you
The one reading this. I want to
Take you in my arms and touch
You intimately, make love with you
With great ceremony and unbridled lust,
To be a chorus within you, not
Singing at all, but speaking so we
May hear in our core, abandoning gender,
Fine and carnal, pleading another kind
Of Summer, another mouth upon yours
Where speech stops attending us
Where all becomes sensation,
Steam rising from the ocean surface
Even before dawn is aware of it.

D.R. Wagner

CAPES AND CLOTHING

She puts on the cape of swans.
She puts on the cape of darkness.
She puts on the cape of dim music.
She puts on the whispering cape.

She has the songs already in the chamber
When she fires. They look for corners
In the night where they may hide as darkling beetles
Do. She puts on the chorus of stridulations.

It is so easy to be distracted, to look away,
To lose sight of her movements. She wants
It that way and drives her car as if it were
A moth finally escaped from the flame charms.

The sea horns begin to make their low pitched
Bellows. "There are dangerous rocks here,"
They announce without any words at all.
Everyone cowers in fear, the sound of the waves

Crashing against the cliffside. Let us hurry.
Bring the instruments. Find where the words
Are kept, what shapes may be noticed in deepest
Night, where the moon is resting right now.

She puts on the hood of stars.
She puts on the shoes of the sylph-footed.
She makes the gestures learned from the old days.
She slips away before we ever get near her.

PRISONERS OF THE AIR

The stands of trees engage
The evening birds like tongues
Of fire. They revel in an electricity
Made of feathers and nervous squalling.

How thick is the atmosphere?
Thin as a dream, swirling blue
One could cover with a thumb
When seen from cold space.

All of life can rise to this ceiling
And no further, prisoners of the air.
Dancing in the colors made from light,
Made from the longing of light
To bend around all things and pleading
For a naming. How can we explain this
To our children? Light upon the oceans?

We walk along the edge of the great seas
Unwilling to drive the required knowledge
Deep into our lungs. Our mouths opening
And closing like fish. We forget how to drown.

The sky breaks open and allows
Us to see the moon and its
Stars through a million clouds
And once again we do not know
Where we are. All of life depending.

D.R. Wagner

PASSOVER

This angel knows my name,
Fits his hands close about
My throat and shows
The edge of the sword.

The hands held out to welcome.
"We are the lambs". We think.
Our fingers touch one another.
It is a greeting or a goodbye.

From here we can see the villages.
We gather their lights to us,
Cut the engine and watch the rain
Begin to fall, water as magic.

There is no angel. There is only
Staring into the air, waiting
For a voice, a breath moving
Through what we know as time.

Green, red, blue, orange, yellow.
Oil slicks that shine like the eyes
Of children watching fireworks.
Such wonder discovered over and over
Again. Rolling over in our sleep
We feel the blood push into our arms.

Oh yes, we rise in the morning.
Oh yes, we make great songs to the lord.
Oh yes, the birds are bells of dreaming
Rung to make the world our glowing shrine.

A HANDFUL OF BLUE STONES

I've seen that little bird before.
It seemed wild but it actually
Lived with the gypsies, never
Quite a pet, always a tall
Tale. It could land on a
Saddle horn while one was
Riding and one would not notice it.

When she opened her hand it
Was full of blue stones. They
Looked like Opal, but
Seemed to have memory. I would
Always be the other in the dream
And have the ability to speak
Ancient languages without knowing
If it would be understood. Other
Dreams careened into me.
They sounded like nightingales
And contrived to find rest for me.

Stop. Please stop.
I asked the sea.

D.R. Wagner

THE JOB

I leaned against the wall,
Slid into a squat and stared at the fire.
The flames looked like toys. They popped
And whistled, made reference to many
Things, nearly forgotten, made new even
As they disappeared into warm ash
Carved on a breeze. Temples of smoke.

We had been working hard. The floods
Were coming and the crests of the waves
Would carry demons, naming the heart
And all it provinces, flooding its every
Room before a breath could be taken,
Slamming the bodiless ghosts together, thousands
Upon thousands of them. We would pick
Up the bodies later, when the lights
Finally returned to the room.

A first star. The sweep of angel wings
Across an infinite stillness.
From here I could look down at all
That was below as from a great height.
The fire. The great waves moving over
Everything. Light going out ahead of the waves.
Nothing ever stopping. Breathing.

CAGED

This one is for the caged hearts.
The crazy ones trapped inside of love
That is unconditional, pacing the floor
Unable to understand the whys of the beloved.
The ones beyond dreams and fantasy
Where the entire field is wild with longing.
Desire in its high boots splashing through the blood
Stream, wanting to touch and embrace but unable
To even move the hands from the sides except to pray.

The ones where morning never comes,
But hangs by threads of flesh slightly out of reach
Holding all that is precious with the teeth, making
One unable to speak clearly, without falling into stupor,
Drunk and enraged by whips and cold chains.
Waiting endlessly for some sign, some warming
Where the breath holds a kiss or a word that says
"It's okay. Everything is all right. Don't worry."

Without being a joke or a cruel twisting of the language
Into confusion and a drowning in memory
That removes the beloved even further from the moment.

Let us pray. says the flickering light,
The waking in the middle of the night,
Cold and unrested, listening for footsteps,
Wanting them to come closer yet fearing
Them still as one would a pack of mad dogs.

D.R. Wagner

THE GOLDEN CHILD

What have we forgotten?
The way back to our room?
The round blue ball covered
With water that we kept floating
In space, spinning it the while?

The little watercolor we used
To keep in the kitchen near the door?
It showed a meadow with a small
Lake just beyond where that fence was.

The field near the woodlot where
Summer could always find us
In the late evenings sitting together.
Sometimes we would talk about
The future as if we might find
Ourselves there someday, still together.

The path to the barn covered with snow.
How anything could look like that,
So white it was almost blue in moonlight.

The box on the top of the dresser.
You said it was for dreams but it too
Has become lost. Perhaps the wind
Knows something of it or that breeze
That comes just now as we fall asleep.
Yes, perhaps it does know after all.

IX

I AM THE MOON

A frightful symmetry
Seen through the leaves of night trees
Just as the moon clears their confines.

I will tell you that this is only your grief
Speaking and that you do not desire death.
You will attempt to argue through drunkenness
And you will leave, sleep dressed as madness
Wraps your brain and stops the parade.

Suddenly the moon cracks open the night,
Filling it with its delicious light.
It plays with our imagination.
"I am the moon,:, it says. "I am the moon."

Most things are without sense.
We make the most of what we have,
Drive ourselves to understand in broken
Cars, demanding the extra mile.

I hear you breathing, but it does not seem
To be a rest, rather, the trough of a wave,
The catching of the moon in a glass,
The surface of a great body, totally transformed.

D.R. Wagner

EPHEBES

In the morning, very rarely, you hear them singing.
The ephemeral is considered luxurious,
Something they do not have to remember,
To reflect upon as one would fantasy,
Without perspective or much interior,
Shallow as mirrors are shallow
But seemingly deep simultaneously.

Misunderstandings are the coin of the realm.
They allow images for only a moment
When an ejaculation may demand its own
Punctuation to show propriety,
Their need of full citizenship
In a society unblessed by complete
Understanding.

We may wander up and down
The streets tempting them to knowledge
Of common things like music made
With the voice alone, or the shaping of glass
Using long, thin tools to play the fire.
There is little interest in these things.

Everything must be prepared well beforehand.
Nothing must be out of place. Where love
Enters is difficult to determine,
A back door, left carelessly unlocked
So one might enter in the middle of the night
Undetected and find a bed with another,
Hoping for a morning that is full of rain
Or fog or other weather that confuses
The senses making everything harder to see.

FLOURISHES

There is a little flourish this wren
Does just before it leaves the branch
For the next one. It is small, so

Small it is hard to see it when it happens.
You, in your way of speaking show me a flourish
That lifts your words just above the edge of
Understanding and tips them into the universe

So they look like an interesting species of butterfly
Never seen here before, never held in the hand.
It can hardly be noticed but I would bet

A blind man could feel it without a cane
Or a dog. There is a kind of dancing the spirit
Allows itself when a real passion for something
Finally finds the room it is supposed
To live in. The heart feels it. It moves air.

The afternoon had been a long time coming.
It got caught up playing with the sun across
The tops of small waves in the pond above
The mill dam and everything got so pretty it
Was nearly four thirty before it realized
There wasn't much left of the job that day.

That's when the passion kicked in.
Long shadows birthed with the heart
Fully extended like a bright wand.
It was hard to see when it happened
But it caused the tail feathers of a house wren
To flourish for the briefest of moments, like your smile.

D.R. Wagner

Our families stretch their blood lines,
Their nets of living and dead upon the
Days, one upon one and suddenly one
Is forgotten, then two, then an uncle
Who was last remembered by a niece
Many years ago because he offered her a
Lovely glass he had found in a small
Store in the midwest. "I believe that store
Is no longer there. Perhaps you will
Like this glass. Look, it catches the sun
As if it is being careful of the light."

For now we will sit on the steps just
Outside the house and allow the moments
To come down around us without purpose
So we might better understand the earth,
Her strange habits, her long, long thoughts.

THE EARTH FORGETTING

We watched the earth forgetting.
There were animals no longer seen,
Gems so brilliant they could create
Silence in the mouths of great kings,
The humming across Summer of insect
Joy, drifting their song above flowers
No longer seen in the draperies
Gathered by the seasons, Whose
Smile was that? and it is gone
Down the street, not part of
Memory at all, a flash, then nothing.

The music of a piano and a concertina
Wrapped in late evening and dressed in
Sharps and flats has gone dancing.
It will not come back. Perhaps
It will be mined from a lost manuscript
Far from now and be seen at eleven o'clock,
But for now, the earth has forgotten.

It is busy counting waves against a thousand
Shores, finding them unspeakably beautiful.
It watches the moonlight on wheat fields
Ready for harvest beneath a full moon
Wondering what color they are, how it
Might be called, if at all. There is
Always more. It forgets the leaves of
A thousand trees and waits for us to
Notice they no longer have names.

D.R. Wagner

CARGOES

Ginger and cotton,
Pistachio nuts, poppy seed,
Nutmegs and raisins,
Muslin, red and gold bolts.

A vocabulary of things.
Our conversation could not
Find words and did not use
Them when they could be found.

A drape of fabric was more
Articulate than talking of its
Form could ever be. Rain
Was always welcome. It made
Great gestures that caused listening
From both of us. We undid
Mornings and stumbled to our beds
Describing with a sweeping hand or
By pointing at the moon behind
A screen of leaves showing only bits
And splatter of the night in
The trees. It was more than enough.
They were our cargos. We took them
To bed with us, our heads swimming
With dreams even before we laid them down.

Breaking and Entering

It will seem like midnight but we are still
Not sleeping. We will not sleep.
Our pockets emptied of the lovely charms
That once meant everything and are now

Smooth stones in grays and dark
Ochres that can fall into the water
And never be seen again for ten
Million years when that land finally
Lifts itself from the sea
And becomes a road, a trail, a path
Leading somewhere that seems both
Vaguely familiar yet full of foreboding.
We will head that way anyway.
It will be the way that seems
Somehow beckoning.

D.R. Wagner

SMOOTH STONES

They will find where all the heart goes
When it must break. They will
Arrive at dusk on cloudy horses,
Hooves wrapped to make no noise.

They will steal into the passes, the canyons,
The long distances where the heart stands,
Sighing toward the fingers of the evening.

It will look like a mission, a tactical
Movement planned and commanded
But it will not be so. It will be
The hands and the emotions reaching
Into the holy body and twisting
Until the whole thing falls down.
First to the knees, then prone upon
The ground, all the sense kicked from
What was its home and breaking the eyes

That nothing may be recognized again
As it once was. All the words
Changed to other meaning. All the
Looks changed with deeper meaning
Undone, unlocked, left to flutter
On the evening, victims of wind.

We will not be able to hide.
We will see the fires coming for miles.
We will hear ourselves disgraced by lies,
Begging the beloved for a moment of sanity
That is not forthcoming. It will go
On without touching one another again.

Breaking and Entering

This well had a peculiar
Property to it. It was impossible
To pump the oil out. It had
To be withdrawn by placing one's
Mouth to the ground of the well and sucking
The fluid from the
Earth. We were the fish,
Our mouths pressed to the breast
Of the earth, our life breath
Drawing up this oil with fish
Mouth and exhaling emerald
Flames that warmed all the
Winters of our youth.

D.R. Wagner

FOLK TALE

When we lived along the edge
Of the sea we used to heat our homes
With a certain oil that burned
With a particular clear green flame.

As children we thought this oil
Came from the fish that were
Our livelihood. Allejandro said
That the green was caused by the
Fact that a type of fish caught here
Shared a common dreaming.

They dreamed they did not live in the seas but
Instead swam through the oaks and
Firs that surrounded our village and
Because the entire fish was pressed
For this oil, their brains gave
Up the green that was the color
Of the dreamt leaves. Maria Xavier said, no,
It was only the food they fed upon
That graced the oil this way.

As we grew we found out that
The oil did not come from fish
At all, but rather from a sacred
Well on the cliffs above the sea.

THE OVERTURE

for Todd Walton

All about the night was starry laden
Walking through the fog about our feet,
The sky so clear the eyes of night could feel
Into our coats and cold light, light our flopping
Hearts as only weather does and we were out for weather.

Tenderly we spread our flesh together to exclaim
The lucid spray of unanswered messages coursing
Across our eyes in meeting each other and are
You the one? Or did we hire someone to dream
For us and leave us alone to find these roads and chance
Encounter one another in someone else's dream.

Would we even understand the place of such a scene?
Would we strip each other naked and pull at our flesh
For pure sensation or find a place of worship where
Few have trod before and names have not yet
Been made for what would happen there?

Waiting. We are merely waiting for the time to come,
For the ropes to be untied, for the hands upon our minds
Guessing what it is we wanted so badly we found
Our way here, not knowing if that is true,
We venture up the hill and crest it just as the moon
Is rising and we can see the others gathered below

Faith and passion, full of their own manifest and singing,
Yes, singing the songs that lovers sing in languages
They do not understand but grasping anyway for the
Pure water running from the words, spilling into the
Night as obsession cleans itself on these blind hearts
Emptying the river of imagination into the million things
We choose to call ourselves when these masks are
The ones we wear. Craving blindness, yet pure visions
We begin the overture once again, all in readiness.

D.R. Wagner

We will have no memory except that we once
Could dance. There are sounds, of course.
The great composers play with our libidos
As with flutes or double reed bassoons. We
Will delight at the tickling the tongue makes
Across the reeds. We will think each note
Is special, is ours alone. It is not. The great

Symphony moves into our loins and our minds.
We are lucky if we can remember who wrote
The theme. The memory for music is always
The most difficult to possess.
We will always salute you.

COMPOSERS

Whatever is broken will remain so.
The universe does not know when
We decide things like broken. It
Just continues to move without regard to
Names and degrees of importance. All is
Equal here. This time I am equal to you.

I will tell you what to be concerned with
When the night makes that noise it does,
Telling us we have no right to be here.

Sparks fill the atmosphere and join our
Language as words of compassion or damnation.
There is no regard for the fact that we might
Have family or that we might be in love with
Someone who is quite important to us. No

Rules here, my friends. The herds of migration
Have no trouble flattening the trails toward
Water or a safe harbor away from the teeth
The sea brings to our voyages there. You
Can place bets but chances are I will have
Sex with those you love and you will have
Sex with those that I love and when migration
Is over we will have no memory at all. Everything
will be the change. Everything will be old again.

D.R. Wagner

"SMILING AT ME AS THOUGH I MIGHT BE VERY YOUNG.'
....K. Patchen

I had my own room once.
No, one time, really. I'd listen

To piano music there and sometimes
Sleep. I had a special place where
I kept a candle, a tall one, that
Was as wonderful as a rainstorm
When it needed to be. Ha. Ha.

I guess I mean when I needed it
To be. Like this: 'There's bears making that
Sound outside. They won't be hurtin'
Us. They just don't know so much.
They have been walking all day. If we
Go out there now we can see them
Leaving the meadow. They were pretty
With that twilight on their fur.
They almost look purple.
Ever see a purple bear?'

VIII

Breaking and Entering

We came here because we must
Come here. We were told this is
The place. Where will love
Go better? Where will anything
Be as innocent as this ever again?

I press my face into her hair
And breathe. They will come
For us soon enough. Don't
Even think of running. Just
Look at that horse. Unbelievable!
The lovely girl, naked. Her beautiful
Back. Look how we understand this.

D.R. Wagner

ORNITHOLOGISTS

They banded a naked girl
Riding a beautiful star specked
Horse with the echo of youth
So they might track her
Should she ever return.

Somewhere out there silence
Can be learned as if it were
An alien language or a card game.

See those spinning lights?
They are the ones I spoke of
In my letter. Yes, they are
The children of of the deepest
Purest thing we could ever imagine,
But we could not realize them
Happening to us.

Now I don't know about the rest
Of you but I'm thinking none of this
Is done in vain. This is the world,
Is it not? "We are surrounded by
Enchantments." Who can judge
Any of this? Moonlight? Lions?

Breaking and Entering

I saw the myriad colors of the rabbits float
In the air. All the real magic was in the beasts.
They were like jewels against the autumn
Light across the steep hill. I had a prayer,
If one can call it a prayer and watched the
Buck rabbit rise up from the ground, golden,

Mount that air and look for a way into history
That, on that day would not involve its death.
I didn't see this until years later. I was already
Middle aged and understood many things
Differently. Rabbits were one of those things.

This is probably a story about angels.

D.R. Wagner

BAWL MOUTH
thinking of Bob Baxter years ago.

And what of the rabbits?
Where were they waiting?
Down below the puddles,
Sitting with wet feet. Stopped.
The dogs would come. Waiting.

The lead hound was a bawl-
Mouthed bitch that didn't have
A mind, only a nose and only
For rabbit at that. She'd never
Run a squirrel or a pheasant.
Her nose was rabbit.

On the ditch the hunters
Decided to walk one to each side,
Running the dogs down the middle.
This would raise any life before them.

Coming down the wind, they smoked
Cigarettes and made jokes about nothing.
Guns at the ready. It was a very small
Life they were after. Who would notice?
The dogs only to be sure.

Now me, I could hear the boys breathing,
Knew they would eventually flush the fur,
Probably add it to the line up of dead
Animals at the top of the escarpment,
A show of prowess and the magic of hunting.

A QUESTION OF VERACITY

Brave little moment repeating
Itself, waiting for the mind
With its fine tigers to parade
Through, earnest in their spectacles
Of calm madness hovering
Along the same roads we travel,
Waiting for the mind, for us
To find the crowded streets
Sweating like skin tattooed
With a symbol that will lead
Us through these same stone
Streets always expecting,
Always arranging them one
After another, as if they could
Mean something more than
The borders of our madness,
Our rush to see them sorted out
Hoping this means we really exist.

D.R. Wagner

DESERT FIRES

When I was sixteen, lean
And bright as a naming,
The clock, round about, a face
Of what's new and yes to everything
False and true, as if it came
Untied with each passing of the hands
And clapped themselves
Before me. Joy, in rising in the morning
full of grace and Hail Mary to the tune
Of Introit bells and Sext and None.
I'd launch myself into each afternoon
As if the world depended on my being there.
In a chair, curled with book and book
Or, off across a blank of lizard
Mesas, undone by sage and the blasting
Light of Albuquerque in July. And I,
Off to see how full of insects such
A day could be or build some secret
Fires in the smallest spaces I could
Find. A ritual of heat within a heat.
White flame inside a ground squirrel hole.
A mouth inside, that said itself, that said
My name. Oh, I was there, alone
And heard the time, slipshod in 50's boots,
Come clumping by on half-marked paths and trails
To catch my neck by scruff and wrest me
To the changes, to landscapes full of burning holes.

Breaking and Entering

She was not given to understand
More of this than her hands covered
With the cool and brilliant light.
She wishes us luck as we continue

Toward the shoreline, the same light
Glinting off the water, infecting
Our minds, making everything in life
A challenge and the turning of the days
Borne on the backs of black birds
Exploding time with cackling and shrieking.

D.R. Wagner

HALLOWEEN

She filled her hands
With winter light and November's
Crows, a cacophony of wings
Against the blue of early evening.

Children used to come here.
There were hills and copses and woods
Challenging the imagination with shadows
Caught alive in stories of the Fall.

The road ended at her mouth,
Full of weeds and drifting terrors
Searching for a body to accompany
During the dark evenings of the waning year.

Shaken, she reaches for the twilight
As if it were a vessel of some kind,
Easy on any sea, unmoved and with sails
Painted in the colors of forgetting.

To dream was to vanish into memory,
The twinkle of an eye,
The brush of a hand across a shoulder,
No place for sharing stories, whispering.

This time of year is full of stuff
Like this, fine of hand and bathed
In a crystal construct made of wood,
Made of fire, made of singing.

Breaking and Entering

We stand at the rail of the boat.
The sea churns behind us, unalarmed
By all of this. In the next second
We remember everything.

I will kiss you like this again.
I will talk to your relatives as if they
Were photocopies of great bridges
That once spanned continents, places
Where we could see what was coming,
Unable to do anything about it.

D.R. Wagner

BREAKING AND ENTERING

Broken glass on the floor of dreams
Cut the feet and blood comes, a memory
Unrestrained and opened like a body in surgery
Runs and seems to be something spectacular.

A walk through a park in Springtime.
Explosions in the inner eye, an inability to
Walk to the edge of reason, love, drunken and useless
To form words, night terrors, adolescent concerns
With appearance and impressions derailed,
Sparks streaming from the mouth.

A sudden reversal of fortune, no way
To stay awake through it all.

We walk to the edge of the abyss.
We say our names to each other.
Nothing makes much sense.

Crickets begin their stridulation and the flesh
Parts below the dermis and works its way
Upwards to where we dine together,
Laughing and kidding about old times.
The way we understood each other.

Finally, splashes of liquids cool the flesh.
We hope they are parts of songs we once sang.
The referee makes arm signals showing
What it is we have done to deserve such penalties.

THE BANNER UNFURLED

We were standing below the eaves
With the rain coming down hard,
Almost unbroken as if the water were
A solid that had been forced to
Reconsider its mission. What was it

To do? Be drunk? Irrigate crops?
Flood a street? Drown an animal?
That and the day around it, gray
With an insistent dull red of the
Traffic light breaking through the torrent
On a predictably regular mission
To change the day with its insistent interruptions.

It was no good. We knew we would
Be here for a long time. The world
Had turned soft and soggy around us.
We were no longer able to talk through
The downpour. I remember thinking "This
Is what it must be like all the time when
We grow old and once again live alone."

I knew this wasn't so but it
Became a banner and I imagined
The years running away from me,
Afraid of what would happen next,
The water rising above my shoes,
Slapping at my ankles.

D.R. Wagner

THE STONE BIRDS

The stone birds shattered
On the tiles just below the garden
Arch. Broken heads, bodies in
Pieces, more still than death is
Able to make us understand. There

Was no blood. It was not a great
Tragedy, just an unwinding, a slow
Unwinding of late morning
As we returned from the hill near
The edge of the sea, from watching the
Morning slide its fingers into the cove
Through the woods. You said the sun looked
As words might have looked had
There been sound beyond the soft
Ticking of the waves into the coolness.

No, it was just the fact they were
Broken. The end of a sentence or
The beginning of a lesson we hadn't
Contracted to understand.

"Raccoons," the gardener said, "They will
Do things like this occasionally. I think
They do it just to see what it looks like,
Just to see what will happen."

THE FROST

Eased onto the window sometime
During the hour of the night
When no one would notice, a glissando
Swirl and feathering rarely more than
Halfway up the glaze and when cold,
A complete tracery, all patterned etching.

There were the broken shells of the
Night, the tracing. The vague
Paths that describe themselves by shadows
And the compass of the moon
Breaking through the trees. Not that
The paths led anywhere.
They were a kind of cadenza to the frost,

Creating its dissertation in water vapor
Defining the infinite beauty of the cold.
The endless challenge of being forever
Creative and the quick dissolution
That even a hand filled with warm can make,
Changing everything forever,
Turning back to drops of water.

GOSSAMER

When the wind decides, it is 'Where
To', that hails its most intimate
Secrets and lays claim to a chance
To make them places.

Here, I will sell you this wind
On a knotted string. These are my
Angels who die as soon as they
Are born. And we will be borne
While waiting atop a quiet post
In the middle of a field that long
Ago ran with black-faced sheep;
Their hooves leaving an indelible
Writing on the sides of hills that can
Be read one hundred years from when
They were steps ahead of the dark,
A list of primal fears as night
Twisted around them.

And yet here we are just before sleep,
Raising our silk high above our heads,
Heedless of whether we will go. Awaiting
The wind and the wind only as it rigs
Our yearning and we do its will.

VII

D.R. Wagner

SMOKING

Well something died or sounded like it
Did. There was a sharp crack, but not
Loud a twig snapping or a glass
Marble checking into another.
The sound became constant.

Then the lurching. It probably was just
Me moving that way but I knew it
Wasn't. I might see it all. The
Difference with which the minutes
Clicked past carrying foreboding
Like a small caliber pistol.

Plus it was dark. I could hardly see
Anything but I knew it was all right,
All correct, all lined up ready to inspect.

Then the words started coming on their own.
They weren't about to stop or claim
Inspiration. They belonged there with
Or without me at the reins.

I retired to the edge of the mesa where
I could look down on the whole thing.
Not away from anything, not connected in any
Way, but so sure of myself I bought a pack
Of smokes and lit them one after
Another until they were gone.

A BROKEN PROMISE

Lying on the ground. I was surprised
To see how much it looked like a mantis
Someone had stepped on by accident.
The elongated body parts, the almost
Transparent wings covered in a green
Sheath, now sticking out from under
The crushed cover. The legs splayed
And unnatural in their direction with
The exception of the praying legs
With their serrated edges, now neatly
Curled close to the thorax.

It was the head that most carried
This illusion. In its expression
And large eyes a huge question
Still there, maybe a surprise at
Suddenly finding itself broken,
Unable to move, unable to accomplish
For some reason that would never
Make sense, but would always be remembered.

D.R. Wagner

THINGS WITHOUT NAMES

Waiting near the rock just where the river
Took a perfect right hand turn one could
See the water moving faster and faster.

As it tried to turn it forced itself beneath
The soft limestone and gradually worked
Holes in the rock above where it would
By force shoot straight up in the air seven to ten feet

Wait a few minutes and do it again. As it did so
Its greater body began to move in a counter
Clockwise direction, seeming slowly but ever
Turning, ever drawing all of water to its vortex

Lifting entire trees caught in the river flow
Straight up. Everything belonged to the water.
Things with no names populated the white swirl
Popping to the surface, then disappearing
Sometimes forever, other times bobbing
In and out of sight for weeks at a time.

The whirlpool owned everything that moved
Within its huge body and played upon everything
In a complicated mystery of change and constancy.

We watched it for years, its slow brooding
As it tracked the rivers profound turn.
No information was ever given by it,
Just the dull greywhite of the water itself
Insisting on all that passed downriver,
Calling every bit of that body its very own.

Breaking and Entering

There was something here she wanted
So to recall but it disappointed,
Not knowing her again, without
Communication, without having
Any name she could recall.

Without a word she remarked
How different everything was this time,
How she would never know me,
How this place would always
Have this kind of memory for her.

D.R. Wagner

A CERTAIN LOST GRACE

By chance I am not you,
Do not carry your name or
Call your mother my own,
But I do understand you, why
You would say what you say
About the oppressive heat causing
The transformers to explode in

A bright pink flash that
Could be felt across the skin
Yet still not be recognized
For what had happened until
The entire neighborhood lost
All electricity and bathed itself
Again in the old darkness now
Mostly unremembered except in

The winter coats dreams use
To ward off mistaken identity.

It is then I remember your
Mother and see her standing
On the corner on a late July
Evening wondering what could be
Keeping memory so long?

Breaking and Entering

These planets in their luxurious fire
And gaze at them without fear
In not knowing what they were
Or why such a thing should be.

They were unelected, like love does
When it finds itself in a depth
It has never seen before, much less
Understand, yet still as true and wide
As the great Missouri River in full
Flood, everyone standing on the banks
Wondering if we shall perish or merely
Break into tiny shards of glass.

D.R. Wagner

TINY SHARDS OF GLASS

We were sitting in the other room,
The one away from the woods.
We were unable to see what was making
The noise but we all could hear it.

We all heard different things.
That it was music seemed a general
Agreement but what clothing that music
Wore was what mystery would come
To claim as a definition.

I was dreaming the form.
Nothing had prepared me for it.
It kept breaking like promises,
The kind made when you're really afraid
And will forget when the light returns
Or the danger passes or we recognize
Someone we know and everything isn't
So scary anymore. It burns.

When I opened my hand there were five
Planets, each in flames, each a different
Color. This was unacceptable
But brought much comfort from the noise.

We had supposed it to be something,
Anything almost, a place to begin,
A room toward understanding but

It was not. It was a mere stone,
A place to stand, to emote and to
Have a place where we could see

Breaking and Entering

I realized this, dismounted and
Walked carefully, step by step,
Down to the sidewalks of a neighborhood
I would truly never be able
To walk again. The wind
Already quickening across the trees,
Cutting through the window, open
Against July and telling me
To "Go to sleep. Go to sleep.
We will take care of everything."

D.R. Wagner

A PERFECT MAGIC

There was a certain throw of rocks
That led out into the lake where
We could stand on the greatest of them
And proclaim wishes to the evening.

We were ten years old. We thought
That wishes were indeed magic and because
Summer was upon us and because
The light that held July for as
Long as it did and glowed on our
Shadowed forms, that this was
Enough magic to allow almost
Anything to happen.

What we did not know is that
This perfect magic, while ours
For this blessed moment, was really our
Gift to those who came after
Us in time and found themselves
In this same place. Our eyes tearing
Across decades to feel their flesh
Again for a brief moment, to sing
A song to them. But it was
Not a song they knew and all our
Efforts were only bird songs just
Before the sun abandoned the place.

CHANGE

Sometimes there is a long thunder
That comes down from the hills.
It seems quite quiet at first, then

Builds, rolling off the tops of the high
Places and tracking across the valley
As if it were a floor of dreams.

Not the kinds of things one normally
Thinks of as dream, but more refined
As if years had taught the sound

Exactly how to lean this way so our
Ears could find the voice there, that
Of rain, that of electricity, that of change.

It was the change that made the difference
For it came without desire, dressed
In plain clothing and limping slightly

As it reached down through the weather
And softened the air for the water.
How quietly it came upon the thunder.

One would think it was something expected
But still surprising in a particular way
Like falling in love or dying.

D.R. Wagner

THE SAND

The sand has the name of the journey
For it has known the seas, can speak
Their names and tell the storms
The secret places where the wind hides
Its stormy jewels and sings its terrible
Songs. Oh the night. Oh the night.

And we hold the sand within our hands
And we let it go between our fingers
Making patterns with its soft body,
Its gleaming eyes, the mantle of
The waves. Oh hear, we die in seas
So cold the ice itself grows teeth
And spells our ship till it
Commands and we, even climbing
High into the masts can see no
Land and fall, oh yes we fall
For twenty leagues and call
One to another across the loom
Time makes with water and here
You came, and they, dear friend,
My dear, dear friend are made of sand
Are made of sand.

KISSING ONE ANOTHER

I cannot make the words turn anywhere
Toward what I want to say. Exactitude
In the tearing of wind through the line
Of trees along the edges of the park which
Absents itself in the lost songs of ancient
Wood, Elm to be specific, Locust, to be a season.

There is no scale. I am lost in the dust that words
Cast upon the walking form of man.
The twilight man. The man about to sit
Upon a chair. The man embarking on
An explanation of form who disappears
Forever in a throng of words ridden
Into oblivion by those who would define
Everything that is said as if it had more than flow;

From staring at a beautiful woman into
An explanation of what the bishop had
For breakfast that turned the parish
Into an unsymmetrical sludge that
Caught itself in prayer and barely
Saved what we know as the final,
The unique, the absolute. Somewhere
We forget exactitude and find darkness
Kissing one another, hoping for ultimate substance.

D.R. Wagner

QUICKNESS

We will hardly notice when this
Is over. A sudden flurry of description
As if a poem were an uncommon species
Of bird that hardly ever visits these
Colder climates, even during the short
Summer days when insects form dense
Clouds in the air and conspire to
Be the noise filling the night. Clouds of them
Blocking sunlight and even the moon
For moments at a time and then
There they are shining again against
The buzzing darkness with its curious

Movement, wings through the thickness
Of the air. The ground littered
With hundreds of thousands of
Tiny winged bodies in the morning
Just as new clouds begin to
Form close to the surface of the lake,
Fish rising through rainbows to snap at them.

VI

D.R. Wagner

THE HAND LIFTED TOWARD THUNDER

Only the span of the hand raised
Against a late weather, the sun down,
Night knowing what it must do,
Drops of water are deflected as a ceremony.

The hand cannot stop the thunder. Thunder
Clings to the outline of the fingers
Like the sea to the shore line.

Every cranny delineated by the lightning
The moment carries with it. Still thunder
Comes against it, forged perfectly
As jewels and ornaments, weapons and shields
Are forged. So quickly,

Mercury bringing it,
Hephaestus smithing. Two brothers
Against the hand for a moment and
Discontented with the silence of words
Inclines thunder toward the world
And explodes in meaning even before
We realize with what we are dealing.

THE SPARKLING DEVICE

That spills over the edge
Of the world as we imagine
Water or song made incarnate;
Rippling with flesh and somehow
Telling tales the while. It is all
Discovery and the opening of the field.

Once again, decades later and still
Chanting Duncan's admonition,
"There is no greater wrong than
To force the song," a flock of
Yellow birds through dappled forest
Light, twitting and a flash of wings.

"Oh we have seen him there," we swear.
"We have and leave off from our task."
I stand and stare even further
Into the forest knowing that we do not
Know what lies there and knowing that
We must go anyway and find that
Water we imagined towering like a
Pillar and astounding the very stars
With its poses and quick stances
Saying our name and asking us to watch it churn.

D.R. Wagner

"A CENTURY OF DOVES"
...Douglas Blazek

A dreaming.
A tearing at the windows
That opens to a particular jewel.
We can walk there. Even the air
Smells sweet as if the clouds were charms.

Here the Forlicon hills seem
To challenge the sea, almost taunt
It with hard, nearly leafless scrub
Plants that never seem to notice
The wind and cold rains. Like truths
That have seen all fools, they never
Shake in their perfect occasions,
At spring, they have the smallest
Of yellow flowers, four-petaled.

I caught it in my throat
And it was a birdsong, one
I did not recognize and I thought
It my own and perhaps I had
Made it and then afraid to look
Down, but doing so, I saw myself
Fully fledged gazing at two pure
White herons perched in the branches
Of a tree nearly submerged in
A pond. There was only a moment of this
And the hills returned around me and I wept.

This might be a story but it does
Have horses. So we might want to
Leave before we know too
Much to begin insisting on a dawn,
A special fire that really gives
Nothing away at all.

And so I think I'm telling you a story
But it seems all about a carnival
That happens tomorrow in a poem
Left in a book so very long ago.

D.R. Wagner

MANHA DE CARNAVAL

I am unable to do anything about it.
I stare for hours at the ocean.
I have been taken. My thought
Listening to translations from
A language made of magic and swift gestures

Captured from dances performed
By a hooded crowd who insist
We know them but they do not
Know time and we show the tattoos
Of time all too clearly.

I am going to walk away from this
For a moment. I am in danger of
Falling too far and becoming water,
Totally water, once again.

I saw spirits moving as clouds
Toward an infinite tomorrow.
I am unable to recall if we arrived
Here to do something special like dying
Or if there was to be a fiesta
That had another ending, a sky filled
With fireworks. We have seen such
Things as we are not allowed to
Even attempt in explanations.

I sharpen my knives. There will
Come a time when a dagger will
Hold all the language, when we
Will garb ourselves for inclement
Weather and find our horses.

WINTER, 1879 - 81
CLAUDE MONET GOES TO WORK

These Winters had been extremely
Cold. Le givre, the frost, covered
Every morning, demanding the Seine
To be still, quieting the landscape
For days. There were no birds at all.

Camille was gone; a mist in the grey*
Swirl that was all of Vetheuil that
Year. There was always the river.
It seemed to carry the most elusive

Of Colors for brief periods of the day.
This was a good place to look at without
Thinking. The ghost trees away, across
This frozen place would become translations.

Painting. The days passing. The ice finally
Moving changing into floes. Painting.
The sun trying to move the season.

Painting denies language and all
Mortal sounds. The Winter mutes
All things further into silence. Years
Later this time will have no appearance
Other than landscape, a view, an object.

It would take many years to paint
The river. The sunsets, the ice breaking
Up finally the coming of the Spring,
The palette changing, the light lengthening,
Apple trees in blossom by the water.

Camille Monet, Monet's first wife died at
Vetheuil on 5 September 1879, at age 32.

D.R. Wagner

PIERRE BONNARD AT LE GANNET - 1932

It was now 9:00 a.m.
The light would be entering
The bath room just now.

The way the trees outside
The window caught this time precisely,
Bouncing it over the walls, mixing
It with the surface of the bath
Water. This was the time to paint.

Over and over again particular
Transparencies in the flesh sustained
Great challenge, stopping time
At every occasion, saturating the room
With trinkets of pale tints, quick
Necklaces precipitated by the season.

Again and again, each time without
Remembering the last, he moved
The paint across the canvas.
Each mark an instant only. This
Time exactly. This time exactly.

He sometimes thought the yellows were
Like singing, then not, then pattern.
The figure moving through them,
Rising, bending, claiming all the space
Object by object. Even once Pouette*
Entered the room, lay down on the rug,
Waiting for Marthe to finish**
Drying herself....Bonnard surprised
At the momentary intensity of his red
Dog, swirled against the grey-blue tiles.

*Poette was Bonnard's dachshund.
**His wife.

Trying to say everything. This is how it was.
This is not remembering. "Here is that
Very chair you see. You are having tea
From that same cup she holds in the
Picture. She was delighted to see how
The painting showed many things she knew.

She has long since died. That
Room you see is no more, even
The building is gone. I come in here
Often to look at the painting.
This is how it was. It is like talking."

D.R. Wagner

1923 AND 1938
EDOUARD VUILLARD PAINTING

It was the rooms that mattered.
They were the weather embracing
The figures, the glitter the spirit
Festoons itself with as it embraces
Time, the objects, the shadows opening
To reveal intimate spaces, everything included.

Washing his hands, Vuillard looks
Into the mirror, into the room,
The walls are covered with paintings
Of paintings, a chance to see
Them as they were, still becoming
What they would be, still changing.

Memory works this way, passage by
Passage. We are in the middle
Washing up, looking into a mirror
Reflecting the entire room, reflecting
An open window, reflecting our image.
This time it has become the painting.
We recognize the figures as reason enough
To make these complex observations.

Breaking and Entering

The night quickly gathered all the
Players in her arms. The wagon
Spun into the open air off
The cliff edge, high above the
Town. Townspeople thought it was
A meteor rather than a discovered
Bit of language working as hard
As possible to become a great
Mystery. Within three-quarters
Of an hour everyone had forgotten the
Incident, only noticing the
Way the crowd took sharp, quick
Breaths and made their way away
From the windows, to their homes
Moving as quickly as possible.

D.R. Wagner

THE FOUNDLING AS SEEN FROM A HIGH OPEN WINDOW

There was something about his breathing,
Quick short breaths, as if a spider
Monkey was doing the breathing. There
Was no way to explain why this was.

He moved with a liquid elegance
Seldom seen in any interior space.
The sky seemed to lift his body
Higher than one might expect just
Looking at him standing there.

The room began to attract many birds,
Way too many birds. The noise was
Becoming overwhelming. It was as if a dream
Had broken away from the great
Cart of dreams somewhere on a high
Path and began to hurl itself down
A road never meant to carry more than
One or two riders at the same time.

I should have warned you this kind
Of thing was going to happen.
That all the principals in the poem
Would be forever without identity,

Tossed over a cliff high up on
A mountainside before anyone
Caught a good look at them
Or could construct any idea of why
This might be occurring at all.

THE TREES LEARN THEIR STANDING

From her unwavering gaze
And rivers, their kindest of moods
From the arch of her eyebrow,
The turn of her lips to smile.

The sun pulling itself above
The greeny hills, spends its
Entire morning looking in her
Direction as do I and the
Birds, the wind, the gathering
Clouds lost there too.

May the night forget its way
This evening. We have this
Cup of time only. Do not
Envy us a few poor words.

D.R. Wagner

STANDING ON THE COMPASS ROSE

The entire world below my toes
Rises up and off I go
High above the lands of snow
When all beneath me cold winds blow
And I finally relax, enjoy the show.

The greatest gift is to die
And our form mutates, comes apart and flies
Our selves back together in a new sky

Where what we were and now are
So far away from changes and we cry
To see ourselves so totally new and sigh
Once again at our strangeness and why
Such a thing could happen yet again.

You will wear me like rain
For I will be the rain.
You will dress yourself in pure light
For I shall be pure light.
You will call me by a name
And I again will answer,
Come to your side and see
The sun just begin to rain
Storm, you running on ahead of me.

V

D.R. Wagner

STEPPING DOWN FROM THE TRAIN

Stepping down from the train I was waiting
For the light to change, arrange itself, explain
Why around the tracks such a simple act could
Remain the most significant. Could it open
Another plane, a door, a hallway, a plaza?

There had been gunfire and explosions all night.
The air was a concerto of volleys and the stuttering
Voices that carried death upon their breath.

We knew we had to move as quickly as possible
Or nothing would matter for much longer. We
Could hear children crying inside of the buildings.
Some of them were burning. The whole place
Was being eaten by shadows and tracer bullets.

'Through here then', a voice spoke and a passage
Revealed itself. We gathered what we could and ran.

What was the smoke of powder and of fires turned
To sky and went from red to pink, tinged itself with blue
That seemed to form afterimages around old buildings.
We could hear what the birds were saying. There was
No sound of battle or of pain anywhere near us. Far
Away we could hear the train once again.
It was leaving the station. We had brightly colored
Packages in our arms. People were leaning from
Balconies. They carried candles and were humming
Songs we knew from childhood. All of this took an
Entire lifetime to happen. This brief telling of it must
Be a container placed in time to hold a lantern.

COURAGE AGAINST THE LION

He will rend your flesh from your bones
And show his red and bloody mouth
Below vacant eyes caught in the thrall
Blood brings to that mouth.

Courage then, for yours is the voice
The beast wishes for speaking.
We are the ones to tell the tale
Of its lordship of the jungle and
The steppes and the plains.

The lion in the desert. This is
His voice then. "Do not touch me.
Look upon my words and see that
My own blood pours from them."

Yes they will heal and I shall be
Once again stalking along with death
As if we had nothing better to do.

All these words gathered here
For the sake of what could be a roar.

D.R. Wagner

From what could easily have
Been a rooftop as easily as it
Could have been a bed, one
Could see the cloisters, the
Cities, the dungeons, even the
Libraries full of their disconcerting
Intersections.

This was supposed to be a help in
Explaining a slight, unusual
Occurrence involving
Touch and an unexpected waking from
What could have been a dream.
It has failed miserably.

WHAT USED TO BE A ROOM

The walls peeled away perfectly.
We were standing in a contrived
Arpeggio of detail birthed
Of knowing too much of what
Was going to be said as soon
As time came to repay its debt
To death. A sudden sucking
In of breath that resides
In familiar things, that is heard
Infrequently, as when loved ones
Disappear or when we notice
Passageways in the countenance
Of a sleeper. Perhaps one woke
Too soon and the fragments of
Waking hadn't all escaped the
Gnawing at the edge of sleep.

The face was still incomplete,
Yet we knew who it was.
Hell, we were sleeping with them.

I found I could lift the
Entire thing with the blade of my dagger
And watch it stumble toward
Some idea of what this place
Had looked like previously.

D.R. Wagner

'What is perfect?' I asked him.
'A lamp atop a three drawer dresser.'
He answered. There are silhouettes
Of deer, squirrels, rabbits, foxes
Birds and the forest in its lamp
Shade. It is perfect.', he said.
'It is also only four inches tall.'

He wept and I could feel
The music of a piano musing
Well after midnight come through
His words. 'What am I feeling?,
I asked, alarmed at this.

'You've never been inside a poem
Like this before have you?

His eyes were suddenly the only
Light in the room.

'Touch the walls here very carefully,
My friend. This thing just ends
And there is no bottom.
Watch what happens when
The words run out.'

BEHIND THE MYTH

He always seemed to walk through
Things, never around them as if the night
Were a huge tangle of objects
Moving like a glacier beneath his stride.

And he would crash through
The surface with each step and
Plunge out of sight, reappearing
With the same crashing of steps.

Furthermore, he seemed headed
Nowhere. Our job was to watch
Him. After all he was our guide.
The old ones called him 'our prayer'

And bowed to him when he would
Arrive late to the caves, cut,
Bleeding more often than not
And always mumbling about
Something he had seen in his journey.

We hardly ever spoke to him
Except to ask common questions:
Would you like more soup?
Are you bringing wine with you tonight?

Except for myself. I had decided
To talk to him as if he were
Not our prayer, but rather a kind of drunk
Wanderer whose job was smashing
Underbrush beneath his feet.

D.R. Wagner

SKY WITHOUT A NAME
...a vision

Say this then, that I have known
You better than waves know the shingle
On the shore of the sea that speaks to
It, at telling of its presence, its golden
Robes, shadows deeper than the memory
China dresses up and presents as a tiger.

Crossing the sky without a name,
Claiming that it is beautiful, while a bird,
A most beautiful bird, a white one
With the head of a wolf pounces
Upon us full of those damned flowers
That keep us from all committing suicide
In the light of such a setting sun
Too incredible to be believed.

Pleasure in a warm young bird.
The sky drifting high above us,
Feeling this on our skin like leaves
That fall on our graves with every hour we linger,
With every star we dare to name.

A SCRIM OF DUST ON WATER
...a pastoral

The sun is reflected but it is tired,
Hours to go before evening is even
An idea. It too is a nomad today,
The shadows on the trees, the cool
Dark beneath the eldest willow, a slight
Lipper in the water and the hopeful
Sound of a bee traveling the dry fields.

Soon it will be show time again
With the leaves beginning to move
In their soft dance, the scrim of dust
On the water breaking up and the sheep
Coming down the slope to loaf beneath
The tree and feel the coolness of the
Water on their dark muzzles once again.

D.R. Wagner

From on high we can watch the doors of perception
Swing open and closed, millenniums of behavior,
Always similar to our own but finally crouching
Behind one another, As flies to wanton boys,
Are we to the gods. They kill us for their sport.

We will leave the room quickly, dress without
Caring, only to be warm, find our way into the snow.
We will get into our automobiles, humming to ourselves
To keep some sanity and drive off into music finally
Done with it, lucky to be alive.

KING LEAR ON THE HEATH

The swarms are moving in. They pass
Through our breath and fog the glass of days
Completely. If they have bones, they use
Them to make music, a curious, dry, music,
The sound of grasshopper wings in a still field.

We begin to write the opera they contain.
"I am more alive than you.", wail the flutes,
Lugging their way through storms and broken
Reed to light upon the quick scarves of the
Tongue and burst into colorful flame, capes
Unfurled, as if they were not paying attention
To how the story might go. They eat heroes
And heroines alike, spitting out the small bits,
Extinct and irrelevant but always catching us,
Making us regret their actions, passing us
With thick arms and buckets filled with fascinating
Treasures from the deepest parts of the sea.

Finally we are asked to walk among them,
Suspend belief, give ourselves over to their
Crackling displays that take language out
Of the senses violently, pulling our hair
To direct us in the direction they will have us
Go. We become weary meeting other people.
Looking for the light in their eyes that allows
Us to understand they have seen what we
Have seen, heard what they have heard.

D.R. Wagner

A PROMISE

I know nothing I could
Want that isn't you.

I've tried, God knows
I've tried, but what
Remains true is that
I wish to touch so
Deep inside all that
I can imagine might be
Yourself as seen or glimpsed
As some mist, beautiful.

A song that only you
Can sing and sing you do
From you to me and me to you.

Breaking and Entering

I seem to speak as you do, drop by
Drop; some clear, some clouded.
I do not know what I am trying
To say. My library pours from its shelves.
Filling all available space, pours through
The windows, through the town and city,
Never stopping. We hardly notice

Where all of language pours back
Into your element, washes itself
Within you and returns to our lips
As we sing endlessly to your mystery.

D.R. Wagner

THE POEM OF WATER

The story is unrepeatable. It has no
Walls but dominates dreams with its
Huge body, so huge civilizations may be lost there.

Never finding their way such a labyrinth
Undoing our tongues by refusing speech
As we open our mouths, no longer able
To breathe, lost once more on our journey
As Ulysses was lost.

I remember the last time standing
on the banks of the Niagara River,
The Upper Rapids.
The rocks seemed to be exploding.
The sound clear and loud but still
We were able to talk to one another.

Then it happens, for over a mile
Eternity opens it mouth so wide
We swoon upon the river banks,
Gazing full into your body.

You are the element.
Oh water that is all things to me
From life, to death, filling my body
With your flowing. Am I in love with you
Or is it that you are in love with me?

Breaking and Entering

The universe may be true for you.
The multitudes exclaim, but if
It is all the same to you we
Will stay here in the safety
Of the verse and rehearse these lines
So that you may understand them
In your deep hearts core
For what comes clearly to the fore
Here is rain. Only rain. Yes, rain pouring its sore
Idyll anywhere it can reach.
For rain is important to poetry
As few other things are
And I have chosen not to talk again of stars.

D.R. Wagner

WE HEARD LIONS ROARING AS WE CLIMBED

Time bends itself around the stars
As if not wanting to consider them
Or consider them other. Balls of gas
Able to flame in a vacuum, sustained
And sustaining, visible and yet almost totally
Unknown except for temperature and composition.
Time had not arrived before those stars
Exclaimed. They could see time come toward them,
A sniper dragging them into a greater sea
Than had ever been considered.

Still the secret was man only.
Alone on his rock gazing into the mouth
Of the lion as he guessed at the stars.

There were too many to consider.
Surely they could not be possible,
Just as this being here to see them
Could not be possible. By then
the heavens were totally undone.
The night filled with sounds of horror.
Sharp teeth cutting into a handful of bones.

I'm not going to bring the stars
Into this again. We already have
Seen love tear into the room,
Disoriented, afraid to open its mouth,
Blowing songs against the wind
So that none might hear the message
Clearly and allow the trace lights
Find their way into our hearts.

IV

D.R. Wagner

TOUCHED BY SOUND

That we could see the place
Where this begins, does not seem
Possible but here it is full of motion,
The light of the movement and the voice that speaks
Directly to you in any given moment.

I have been looking for that moment
The spirit of the dead build
Their chairs behind me and allow
Me to see my brothers and sisters,
Even this late in the evening.

I sing their songs to them and light
Seems to blow across every movement.

I haven't got a chance to stop
In the middle of the story,
Try to remain perfectly still so
Sound may touch me, clutch me to
Its sorry breath and try to change
My mind about how this is thankless work

And we are more than a brief storm.
We pick up our saddles, grasp the moment,
Ride forever.

Breaking and Entering

My bed was rich with coverlets,
Embroidery festooned and as I
Laid my body down, these keen
Women curried favor of me with
Bright singing and the telling of tales.

I must have been dreaming

For I never speak this way
Or feel a longing such as this
For things I have not seen.
Yes, I prick my finger and blood flows.

I must have been sleeping.

And each minute seems an hour
Long and those who sleep cannot
Make songs like this, with
Plays made of glances and of
Gestures only.

I find my boots and pull them on.
I must have been dreaming.
I will write down the song.

D.R. Wagner

I MUST HAVE BEEN DREAMING

I must have been sleeping.
The way through the forest was
Wandering and I could not see
The distances before me.

I must have been sleeping.

The palace is of a fine pink stone
And rises with many turrets.
Banners of colored silk flame
From the rooftops and golden
Eagles coursed above them calling
To one another.

I must have been dreaming.

I had been given one hundred crowns
To find a present for my father,
Who was king of some far away
Country, reigning over many
Wonderful islands. This was to be
Their story or so I had been told.

I must have been dreaming.

The women wore veils and were comely
With ways that moved one from one's blood
When they struck their small harps,
Did their pleasant dances in the great hall.

I must have been dreaming.

Breaking and Entering

Is this the first time you've
Heard about this?.
I am a headful of birds
Endless flocks, thinking of you.
Come join us. Make this come true.

I have been told not to imagine anything else.

"I may take some time on my way.
And I may have to spend some
Time, downstairs."

D.R. Wagner

SWIFT AS THE WIND
for Mike Heron

Inviting the bears in.
Living with wolves.
The light slips in under the door
As if it had serious intentions
To inspire something truly wonderful
When it took the room.

I have no idea where the music
Was coming from. It hit the back
Of my head. I will not be ruled
By such music. There must be
Something more.

The starlings come by the thousands,
Flying their incredible patterns,
Cross-patterns, murmurations
Of ecstasy and confounding all
Understanding into pure magic.

***

Please excuse me. I have just
Been informed that I am the one
Who will carry the weapons.

Do I love you?
Yes, I love you.
All this talking or just words in
The rain? Oh Christ. Oh Christ.
I can't look into your eyes again.

Breaking and Entering

We dwell within the temple.
Do not be alarmed that we have
No corporal body. The light swings
Within us and at long last, at
Long, long last, the voice of the bell
Is ours and is yours as well.

Rise from your simple bed.
Bow to the breath that is your own
And we will bow to you. Bowing.

D.R. Wagner

LIVING IN THE TEMPLE

We were living in the temple.
The ring within the bell
That would never be struck.
The rising of a thousand prayers
On their way to protect children,
Heal those with illnesses, quell the fears
That stalk the dark of forests,
Wished upon the stars and could
No longer kiss the lips of lovers
So far away the sea seemed small,
Tender as a kitten and pounding with life.

We were pounding with life
Were living inside the temple,
Held aloft by incense smoke and chanting.
Om Mani Pad Me Hum, more times
Than the world had turned and we
Had been the ones who turned the world.

Look for us on mornings,
Our throats full of dawn liquor.
Look for us in the stillness
Of the afternoons, in the slow opening
And closing of a butterfly's wings
Resting on a hyacinth or lilac.

Look for us in the last of evening,
Still within the temple waking
Lavenders and reds, crouching on the edge
Of moving storms, poised to become night,
To be the rain against your windows,
The wind within your body.

They are as far away as daylight
Is now and you can touch the night
In pursuit of them them and will never
Reach them until you see
They are not other than your own
Selves. See them glow."

It has been millions of years
Since that night when we saw
The small fires and we are
Still part of the night, but now
We are the lovely fires and
Tonight you find us before you
And think, once again, you have
Seen small fires flaming in some distance.

Wait until that same moon rises
And listen to her sweet words
So that this tale need not be told again

By yet another poet left here
At the edge of night gazing into
The darkness, thinking they are mystery

When they remain only yourselves
Talking to yourselves, for this is how
The soul speaks. How you choose
To hear, will be your own journey.

D.R. Wagner

THE SMALL FIRES

The small fires began to appear
Almost as soon as the sun had set.
Most of them were on the other side
Of the valley. They weren't any larger
Than heartbeats, but there were plenty of them.

They had little smoke about them
But they were bright. We began
To make our way toward them.

The longer we walked toward them
The further away they seemed to be.
They never diminished in brightness.
We continued to walk. The moon began
To entertain us. It twisted in the sky,

Tossing moonbeams all over the landscape,
Lighting the lairs of the bear,
The wolf, the lion, the sleeping elephants
Standing full in the night air with their
Long dreams of endless grasslands,
Caught for a moment by the playful
Slip of moonlight across their gray heads.

I saw the rabbits dancing on their hind legs,
The gathering of night spirits
In circles of ancient trees.
"What are these lights that do not
Come closer to us?", we begged of the moon.

"They are your own poor souls which
You can see and feel but never
Reach. For you do not recognize
Them as the same as you are.

Breaking and Entering

The last time we saw him he was standing in his yard,
Tracing one of his labyrinths out in the dirt beyond his lawns.
Every time he would make it mark, the ground would glow
For several minutes and then settle down.

"Why does it do that?", I asked.
"Because it traces a way home.", he answered.
I have thought about this ever since that evening.
I remember he said that if I would like to see
Something like that again, I must look to the stars.
I have never failed to do so since that time.

D.R. Wagner

THE ARCHITECT OF LABYRINTHS

He used to make bonfires of the stars,
Heap them up in great piles, stuff newspaper
Under them and light the entire business up.
They would burn for hours, blazing away and popping
Comets and fiery cinders high in the air.

Father would let us stay up late on those evenings.
He felt the architect of labyrinths was a magician
Capable of stunning tricks and illusions.

We visited him only twice that I can recall.
His home was small and packed tight with books,
Maps, pictures everywhere and piles of drawings.

He wore a ring on his left hand with a large stone
That looked blue and then looked red depending
On something I could not determine. I recall he called
Me over and asked me to look at the stone, which I did.

There was a tiny hole in the middle of the ring. He asked
Me to look closely at it. Inside the ring I saw an entire
Village, at night, with twinkling lights and people strolling
Up and down the streets, greeting one another. There
Was a kind of music in my head as I looked at it.

"What is this?", I asked.
"It is your imagination.", he said.
I was too young to say anything other than
"Oh." It seemed like magic to me.

TALKING WITH A SPIRIT

You don't have any idea at all
Why you are here, do you?

Other voices leaked into the house.

Downstairs they began to fill up the room,
Staining the furniture and making it
Impossible to descend the stairs.

Say something, anything please!

Is this really the last time
We will speak with one another?

D.R. Wagner

Coming from the front lines. I saw a dead
Man yesterday. They carried him from
The sands back to Pasadena.
He always loved Pasadena.

Gunfire continues in the neighborhood
For awhile until the blue police arrive."
"They know what is going on.
They have the weapons to combat
This madness."

Motorized robots are deployed.
They explode nondescript boxes
As if they were bombs. One of them
Contains parts of a doll and
A ceramic coffee cup beautifully
Decorated with scenes from
A Midsummer's Night Dream.
I pour myself a cup of coffee.
Puck appears at the bottom of the cup.

He seems to be severely wounded,
Crawling toward an entirely different
Morning than the one we had imagined.

"Hello everybody.
Welcome.
When the moon comes over the mountain,
Every beam, brings a dream dear of you."

*

Ramon puts the motor in reverse.
"It's too close to morning now.", he says.
"We don't want to get any nearer. Look
At all the beacons. I wonder what can
Be going on?"

VIGIL NEAR THE ISLANDS

We had never been this close
To the islands before.
There had always been something
That kept us away, that tore
At our consciousness, made us sore
To even consider moving near their
Cluster of beacons.

*

The moon is crippled. It can't
Tell us what to do anymore.
We will be able to walk again.
We will be able to pick the moonlight
Up in our silvered buckets
And bring them back to our
Pillows in the morning.

There are no forgotten rooms any longer.
There are no silhouettes of people
Coupling inside of blank hotel rooms.
These have become cartoons
For the spirit as it contemplates
The process of being abandoned by youth.
There are no explanations left.

Someone picks up an icepick or a gun.
"Remember this?", they inquire.
And we can only recall the
Sprinklers coming on a 1:06 in the morning.

"Are you having trouble sleeping dear?"
The lyrics of the song intrude
On these blood dreams.
"No.", we reply "Look, from where
We are we can see the smoke

D.R. Wagner

Birds perch in the words.
Rivers course through the stanzas
Making patterns between words
As blue as time, as quiet
As boats tethered to the edge
Of the sea. Red and green boats.
Yellow and orange boats, one as
Blue as time.

When we peel the words away
From the page, shadows run
To the margins expecting the change,
Person, plural, definite article,
Contractions, states of being,
A complete suspension of order,
Everything crowded to the very edges.

FIGURES ON THE EDGE OF THE POEM

"And we put confusion on their borders
Until the night was in their eyes."

As blue as time.
Lavenders, electric blues,
All float toward the center
Of the room. They vibrate,
Tremble then move toward one.

There is no self-awareness
Even as we sit down at the table
So close to dreaming one can see
Sleep in the reflections,
In the wine bottles and small
Plates that seem to swarm
The surfaces of the table.

"Would you like some more
Cheese or perhaps the churros?"

A cat occupies part of a shadow,
Declining to be recognized as any
Part of any scene described.

The entire room is built of reflections.
There is no up or down. The light
Passes through everything as easily
As we walk from room to room.

D.R. Wagner

A VISION BEGINNING WITH TAR

The tar was burning.
And I had this vision
About the Christ child
And he was so beautiful
And he could talk to anyone
And explain things that were
Impossible to understand,
Why people played their radios
Real loud on one arm or
Suddenly were compelled to
Use firearms on their families,
Or how lieder evolved to contain
The soul enough to make
One weep, or why there was
Misunderstanding at poker games,
Even when people were not drunk.

And all the while he talked to
Those sweet angels, you know,
The ones you see in paintings,
Would continue singing real
Loud so it was hard to hear
Anything he said and he would
Get on his motorcycle and take
To the back roads, turning north
Out of Auburn and suddenly
Appearing in Nevada City with
A little globe made of gold,
A cross on top and say, easy
As you please, "Peace be with you."

III

D.R. Wagner

It's my wings., I said. They have
Finally grown back but won't
Be of any real use for a month or so
Are you one of them now?, she asked.

No love, you are. Don't touch
Your body except when you
Want to feel the fairy stuff.
No one will believe you anyway.
And it's hard enough to go out
At night alone because you
Will begin to glow all the time.

No. I won't.
You are glowing now. I replied.
Do you know any of their songs?
Yes, I do., I replied.
Sing me one.
They go like this.

EATING FAIRIES

"What are you looking at?" she said.
Zero. I said.
Just zero? she said.

I caught one of them in the garden
Tonight. It was pretty. It had four
Wings and made a musical tinkling
When I held it by the wings.

What did you do with it?, I asked.
I bit it in half to see what it
Tasted like, she replied.

It was better than a frog but I
Don't think I'll do it again.
They are too pretty.

Did you know your mouth has
A glow about it. It looks like
There is light inside your mouth.
Your lips are a gold light.

Don't eat the fairies, I said.

I'm sorry, she said. I really am.
We don't have them near our
Homes and I thought they were
Wild things.

You have too much owl in you.
I said I was sorry.
You'll begin to talk like them
Within a fortnight., I announced.
I can already see you look
Different., she replied.

D.R. Wagner

A SINGULARITY OF CUNCTATION

This time a black hole
That never quite arrives,
Seeing the bridegroom approaching
The tabernacle, splendid in raiment,
Always in view, confident in step,
Yet never arriving, never making
A sound as the rain comes upon it.

However, it is crooked,
Unable to find definition,
Only conjecture used as a reminder.

Still we are changed by this, just moments
Before we reach the age of reason.
Garbled, for sure, but well within belief.

A child would call it a grasping at straws
But children know little of straws
Or other behaviors. We, you and I, find
A clarity in rain and claim of courage
For its even appearing in any such formula.

A SMALL DRAWING OF A WEST WIND

This becoming. This time without sound.
Not a place ever mentioned, not
In books or pointed to on a chart
Clear as can be, describing depths,
The location of sea mounts
Where schools of silver fish
Have been noted by people
Long dead who fished here

And heard the voices of babies,
Children even, with no land in sight.
And drew measured arcs across
The notations of the currents.

This one drew a picture of what
He hoped would show a generally
Following West wind, but with eyes
Too sad to account for such a thing.

I cannot remember how we came
To these places. And now, back again
To the exact spot we were before
But with the total lack of sound, a lack of doors.

D.R. Wagner

THESE ARE DOORS

Tonight I could see them coming.
I could see their embroidered waist coats,
Their high, polished boots that
Reached to the knee and their
Flashing helmets with strange
Designs attached to the top of them,
Designating something important
To them as they rode their
Memorable horses close against
The gates, a kind of vanity
Only discovered when one is driven
From the back rooms of the heart.

They didn't like to be noticed.
They were without history,
Made of oblivion with no index.
We would always see them
Through another's eyes,
Like poems written by warriors,
Nourished by heroes whose deeds
Were limitless.

Still we could hear them moving
As if they were mysterious trains
Remembering dreams, but unwilling
To unleash the multi-colored ribbons
Borne by such as this music is made.

They would have us understand
For a moment only, so we imagined.
They used up years and they used us up
As we tried to unwind their riding,
Back to the realms from which they came.

WATCHING FOR THE CHANGES

We have lost count by now.
There have been many days
Where the things that happened
Were made of such similar cloth
That even death had to unfold
His list of names and loves and
Places fighting had taken place.

But not so much as a rusted steel
Blade remained that could
Speak to how important it all
Seemed in the heat of an argument.

And even death was forced to prop
Up what was left of memory
With tree limbs tied together,
Placed at the edge of a field
Now planted with corn and settle
Everyone down to hear a story again
That they already knew,

Made bright against the row
Upon row of corn stalks and the night
Excusing itself to go about its business,
All the language left to insect voices,
Wind over the landscape and a quick
Stream of hurrying water, hoping
To get past this place as soon as possible.

D.R. Wagner

THE SCIENCE FICTION AND HORROR LIBRARY AT NIGHT

I suppose here, a coolness,
The imagination might insist
Upon, claiming years of adventures
Dante and Quixote, Dunsany and Bradbury.

All shades this cool, unflinching
Evening that begs to know the night
Even more intimately through Patchen,
Hodgson, Clark Smith and Lovecraft,
Himself hiding behind a floridness of language.

I make my way down the stairs,
Well past midnight to investigate
A sound purloined by supposed spirits
And find rows of books out of order
And awry and wonder if it was
Indeed the cat or just the crowding
That some imagination might do
Just to show me it is an attractive
A mistress as any sweet-fleshed body.

I will wait till morning to pick
Them up again and put them in order,
Reading the titles of the stories,
Feeling the cool of the evening
Sifting in and out of the very words,
Imagining everything but the perfection
Of their voices scattered throughout my life.

THE OPERATIONS OF THE MAGIC

You are my dreamer. Today, I am
Without form and you must lift
My limbs and have me climb
The purple cliffs and high places
Far above the sea so that we might
See the glittering cities of the plain
Opened like jeweled boxes against our poor
Wonder. These castles are never to be
Mine. They are yours and yours alone.

You are my dreamer. You are the vehicle
By which I am done and undone.
You are the seas, seas with the
White of the day, seas, here
To show both wolves and the
Soft thighs of a lover standing
By her horse contemplating what
I pray is a unique and untried future
Rather than the twilight of
A fading past. You are my dreamer.
Give me the morning and the day
And the evening once again,
Standing in the finest of lights.

D.R. Wagner

AN ODD ISLAND OF SWANS

They float so recklessly above the greatest
Memories and as an infinity of books
Might have, had there been
No symbols, no heroes, no rules governing
All the theologies witnessed
By water in its myriad forms,
Finally finding Adam standing in the cool
Shower we have come to call prayer.

All this pushed aside to reveal a particular
View from the room of a sorrowing
King to reveal an odd island
Spilled across the top of the morning
That has been required to be your last,
Without ever having been consulted by
A solitary God, unhidden in the voice
A prayer might hope to hold as it stalks
Along the paths beside the ponds deciphering
The wakes and the dark voices of the swans.

ONE ROOM IS A HOUSE

Creeping out among the branches
To know your name. I am above you now.
This is like breathing.
The support we feel when
We recognize our name on
A list of things that may be
Eternal, a whispering in a hallway
That we do not understand.

We watch the lightning strike
The trees in the garden,
The fountain. Oh who will tell
Me if I am dreaming?

I look through the long lists of the saints.
They had no idea at all if they were
Dreaming. I discover my face
In a book of rare engravings kept by
The captain of a long ago disappeared ship.

D.R. Wagner

A POSSIBILITY OF BREATH
for W. Stevens

This space between here and the clouds
Seems careless but for fleeting beauty
And a wharf for docking weary eyes
To something not covered with the dust.
A dreamt majesty that doesn't
Stare but remains an argument
That there is a sweet, staring
Distance between all things.

Waking as we do from whatever
Uncertain depths we
Direct ourselves in so-called sleep,
We find the wide heaven,
This sparkling haven where we no
Longer need make choices
But use the energy we have gathered
To quell time's complaints about
Everything that is not dead,
Forgetting even our own names,
Living here without bodies to see
'The low owl plummet, rising of the morning.'

II

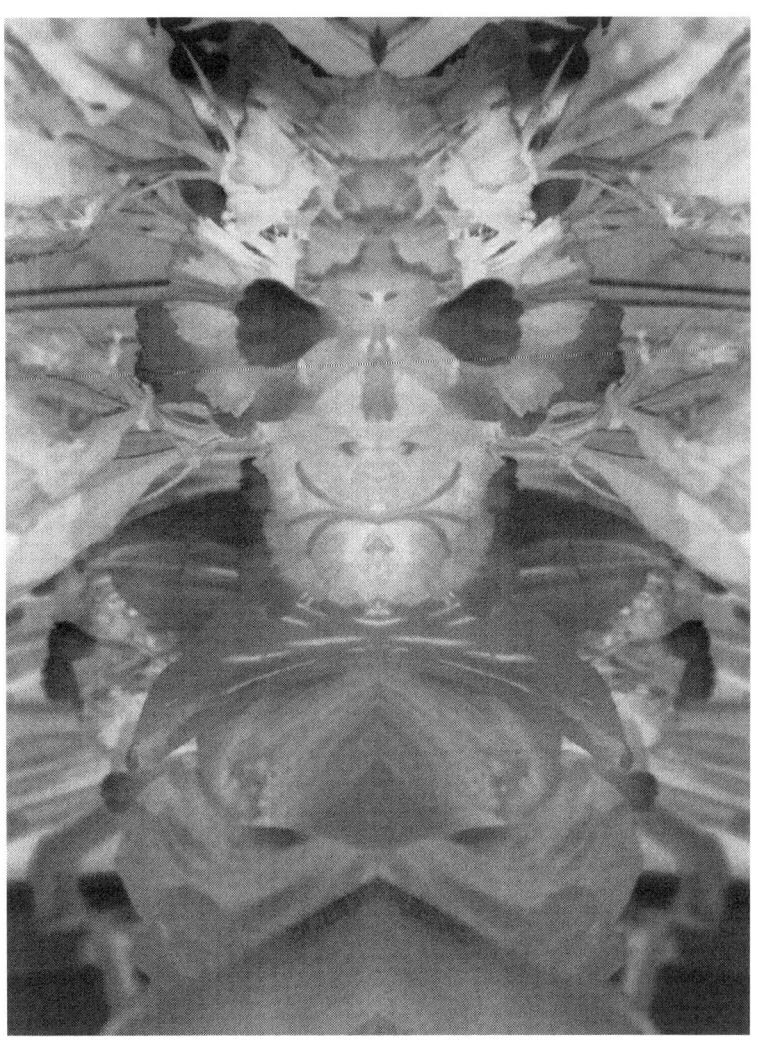

D.R. Wagner

HOLES IN THE SKY

When I pressed myself toward waking
I discovered that some of the rooms
Of my dream had been eaten away,
Large chunks had gone missing.

The parts with the steep steps leading
To the sea, the twilit room where the
Lady sat crying, holding the long-tailed lamb,
The hills where one could see how large
The fires were as they swept toward the towns,
Nothing on earth able to stop them.

A hunger was left in my bones because of this.
I could hear a historic wind wind through my skull
As I reached for coffee, searched to find where
The window looking upon the fields had gone.

Holes in the sky, something peering through
Them from speechless realms, carrying weapons
The likes of which I had never seen before,
Clouded with forgetfulness and trailheads that
I had seen once in youth that had been stolen,
Used to make fires to cook food upon, the smell
Of roasting meat swelling the morning air.

And now this, an aching within my body
Overarching all but the eyes of the highest
Hawk, the screeching bird, seeking thoughts
Smaller than voles to feed upon and I tried
To run back to the sheds of sleep and the coolness
Of streams hurrying down the hillsides
Eager to see the sea, to join the endless tides.

A CHANCE ENCOUNTER

A primitive land that leaves
Nothing much behind. It owns
The Winter sky and displays it
In the dance a willow tree
Chooses to describe a wind.

I would try flight but who would
Understand? Even the birds do not
Know why and it is not everything
To them. Huddled close to a tree
Trunk, knowing when the wind departs
It will once again be time to find
Seeds just beneath the snow.

They have black heads and blacker eyes
And carry maps made of their bones
That tell them where to go.

So I, come here late and without guile
Still detect a primitive ecstasy in
The noises of the crows, the impatience
Of the weather, the scolding I endure
From all imagination for calling this reality.

D.R. Wagner

BASKET CASE

Music in a basket, taken to make a room
And then a dwelling and then a palace.
It has proven itself to be no
Architecture for living. There is no
Inside. The rooms are beautiful
But without doors. There is only
Sound at the end of an arm or a
Stepping across a threshold trying
To direct the forward motion of the whole
Thing.

We live in the crescendos and
Diminuendos. Legato to the
Edge of the cliffside
To see the view and there,
To once again discover the
Woven basket,
Capable of any season,
Full of song and placed beside
The clearest water of a Spring.

CANTICLE DESCRIBING WONDER

Who was it joined the hurricane
To the canticle describing wonder?
Clipping it to centuries long gone
And a hand constantly thought of
As a tree pulled from a landscape
Martyrs might enjoy, notes torn away
From the piano, working temporarily as birds.

A glittering air formed of an immense poetry
Where nothing appears but a singular
Consciousness in the form of an umbrella,
A green mind, then changed by metaphor
To a clear spot in the forest loaded
With medieval trappings and a presence.

A bell-like sound across the square
Where we sit on green chairs
And pretend to be waiting for something.

We watch the hurricane unlock itself
And deliver a blank wall of pure rain.
We have forgotten all about words. We join
Hands and sway side to side, humming.

D.R. Wagner

A LATE JOURNEY

We passed the house of the avenging angel
With its parapets and ribboned trumpeters,
Purple and red-violet the color
Of their eyes. It was the hour
When dreams are captured, sorted
And released to the children born
To the damned and to those who
Wander. They are unable to speak,
Dress in cassocks and flowing
Gowns. They do not take bodies
Often as it is this dreaming
That gives voices to the winds.

We can see a sameness in the eyes
Wild animals turn toward us
When we encounter them in the forest,
Unexpected and interrupting their precision
We like to call behavior.

The stars wound round him, this lurid angel
As the singing rose around us. Lights began
To go out as stars became the evening.

A CONVENIENCE OF CHAOS

The honeycomb keeps the tally
In an even, golden blood, once
Held in the mouth of every
Beautiful worker bee that plies
The structure and its liquid gifts.

*

I found wolves in my heart.
Their white and shining teeth
Pushing past the bone to explain
To this heart that it was
To be discovered, made part of the wolf.

I was forced against the most
Beautiful pine tree I have
Ever seen and felt the white,
White teeth open my thigh and then
The symphony of the pack was upon me.

Ribs turned to bleached instruments
From which music has fled
Except for the coldness of a great
Howling across ice fields and
Thick-crusted snow.

D.R. Wagner

THE VANISHED MAGICIANS

I am still waiting. I gaze from the window
Past the mirrored room, over the terraced roofs,
Looking to the columns of thick dust that rise
In long streamers far away near the river bed.

The water is almost gone now. Most of the people
Have left on their own odyssey taking their cattle
With them. They are looking for an everlasting name,
An infinite domain. We used to think them
Magicians but today they have become fools.
All knowledge of them scraped into a few
Lines of poetry populated with unicorns,
Twisted pieces of iron and an almost imperceptible
Clearing of shadows that is neither
Exaggerated or completely powerless, but which
Exhibits all the marks left by time
On the night sky. They will not be back.

And so we remain here with our over-inventive
Dreams penned up in abandoned corrals
Awaiting a new star, an insistence that details
Have changed, that there will be enough to eat.
We wish for good fortune to accommodate us
Here on the extremes of music,
Prayer and a crumbling spoken language.
I reach out as far as possible.
I am able to touch the soft fabric of the moon.

Breaking and Entering

Or Cervantes, in his study
Watching Quixote re-mount his horse
And totter toward the horizon still searching

When it probably only meant going to sleep
At that particular time so that he might
Continue writing in the morning.
But there still was that damn
Music that constantly needed explanation.

D.R. Wagner

A POISONED LITTLE ROOM

The chanting was coming from somewhere.
It had that lonesome place feel
About it that clusters toward an Orthodox
Byzantine room. The soft gold glow
That time acquires when the sounds
Have almost disappeared. They are
Patched together like years.

A sense of compassion allowed
Itself into his eyes.

A poisoned little room
Cool with basso profundo clicks,
The kind vinyl used to make
When a needle scratched across
Its circular ruins, each song
Dreamed again and again.

Thick stalks of perennials peeled
Back to expose the pith and
A myriad of insects who
Were required to dwell there.

Today I would guess it was a kind
Of cursing rhetoric that could
Be heard and understood as a deep
Disappointment in a mistaken higher power
That lost its name just before one
Completely blacked out,
To wake up in a morning full of ditch water
And a kind of exquisite, misunderstood
Ecstasy John of the Cross
Might have tried to describe.

BESIDE THE SEA

These flowers burn my hands
As they are delivered to me.
I must have gone out at some
Point to gather something like them.
But they became too many bouquets,
Too many different ideas of what
Time allowed me to find. I am
Sure it was for time's amusement,
Just as it finds so many literatures
To poke at as one might a jellyfish,
With a stick, between tides.

This then, is between tides.
I will be patient with it all
And carefully map out the
Labyrinths, make deliberate choices,
Find a mysterious object, half-buried
In the sand, carefully lift it, turn
It over, only to discover a perfect mirror.

D.R. Wagner

ON THE BLUFF

Death was camped out on the edge
Of a bluff under some cottonwood trees..
His horse was without saddle
And was munching grass just at
The edge of his campfire.

What are you doing here death?
I asked, somehow surprised but
Not at all afraid.

Taking in the night, listening to
Bach on my music player, remembering
My work, or part of it.

And you?, he said, are dreaming. I have
Nothing for you yet. You could
Stay here and look at the
Stars with me.

Thank you, but no, dear death.
I am traveling this night to
Escape the heat of the desert.

Dream on, said death, See you
Soon enough.

I

X Radio *134*
Nothing Vanishes *135*
Lips Pressed Together *136*
Copper *137*
An Ancient Battle *139*
Misunderstanding *140*
Crucible *141*
Steps *142*
Chime *143*
Looking At The Life Of A Friend *144*

Acknowledgments *145*

About the Author *146*

VII
- Gossamer 88
- The Frost 89
- The Stone Birds 90
- The Banner Unfurled 91
- Breaking And Entering 92
- Halloween 94
- Desert Fires 96
- A Question Of Veracity 97
- Bawl Mouth 98
- Ornithologists 100

VIII
- "Smiling At Me As Through I Might Be Very Young" 104
- Composers 105
- The Overture 107
- Folk Tale 108
- Smooth Stones 110
- Cargos 112
- The Earth Forgetting 113
- Flourishes 115
- Ephebes 116
- I Am The Moon 117

IX
- The Golden Child 120
- Caged 121
- The Job 122
- A Handful Of Blue Stones 123
- Passover 124
- Prisoner Of The Air 125
- Capes And Clothing 126
- Ceremony 127
- The Clothing Of The Morning 128
- Building 130

IV We Heard Lions Roaring As
  We Climbed 44
 The Poem Of Water 46
 A Promise 48
 King Lear On The Heath 49
 A Scrim Of Dust On The Water 51
 Sky Without A Name 52
 Behind The Myth 53
 What Used To Be A Room 55
 Courage Against The Lion 57
 Stepping Down From The Train 58

V Standing On The Compass Rose 60
 The Trees Learn Their Standing 61
 The Foundling As Seen From
  A High Open Window 62
 1923 And 1938 Edouard Vuillard
  Painting 64
 Pierre Bonnard At Le Cannet 1932 66
 Winter 1879-81 - Claude Monet
  Goes To Work 67
 Mana De Carnaval 68
 'A Century Of Doves' 70
 The Sparkling Device 71
 The Hand Lifted Toward Thunder 72

VI Quickness 74
 Kissing One Another 75
 The Sand 76
 Change 77
 A Perfect Magic 78
 Tiny Shards Of Glass 80
 A Certain Lost Grace 82
 Things Without Names 84
 A Broken Promise 85
 Smoking 86

viii

Table of Contents

I
On The Bluff 2
Beside The Sea 3
A Poisoned Little Room 4
The Vanished Magicians 6
A Convenience Of Chaos 7
A Late Journey 8
Canticle Describing Wonder 9
Basket Case 10
A Chance Encounter 11
Holes In The Sky 12

II
A Possibility Of Breath 14
One Room Is A House 15
An Odd Island Of Swans 16
The Operations Of Magic 17
The Science Fiction And Horror
    Library At Night 18
Watching For The Changes 19
These Are Doors 20
A Small Drawing Of A West Wind 21
A Singularity Of Cunctation 22
Eating Faries 23

III
A Vision Beginning With Tar 26
Figures On The Edge Of A Poem 27
Vigil Near The Islands 29
Talking With A Spirit 31
The Architect Of Labyrinths 32
The Small Fires 34
Living In The Temple 36
Swift As The Wind 38
I Must Have Been Dreaming 40
Touched By Sound 42

When I was a child I believed in visions. Even as an adult I kept insisting the impossible was acceptable. A tiger was in my grandmother's basement, the one I was fleeing from.

In D.R. Wagner's collection, a reader wants to flee into his visions. Find that tiger. It is with the epitome of grace and magic that these poems align themselves with our inner kid, find such realities that only dream worlds can make true. Here darkness can be dazzling! The password is letting it happen. Wagner does this for us.

—*Ann Menebroker*

* * *

"D.R. Wagner's poems launch the reader into a familiar yet uncharted sky. Emotional galaxies introduce themselves."

—*Meg Pokrass*
author "Damn Sure Right,"
editor for Frederick Barthelme's New World Writing

* * *

D.R. Wagner's latest harvest of poems is filled with the brooding sky of a brilliant mind and all its art: poetry, of course, music, and the devil of painting. Everything is here in **Breaking and Entering**. Just hold the book; it will become you. Wagner's fantastic worlds are yours to roam: fearless, curious and elementarily dangerous. You are meant for this – a long vista with the shadow of ecstasy thrown like a scarf on the shoulders of the celestial.

—*Viola Weinberg*
Inaugural Poet Laureate of Sacramento, California
Glenna Luschei Distinguished Poet

This book is for

Lisa

Gabrielle

Annalesa

©2013 D. R. Wagner

©2013 Michael Robert Pollard *(cover artwork)*

©2013 D. R. Wagner *(photographs between sections)*

All rights reserved. No part of this book can be reproduced without the express written permission of the author, except in the case of written reviews.

ISBN 978-1-929878-42-0

First edition

PO Box 5301
San Pedro, CA 90733
www.lummoxpress.com

Printed in the United States of America

Acknowledgments

Much of this work appeared in *http://medusas kitchen.blogspot.com*, an online blog and one of the very few places I send my work to be published. I encourage you to visit the blog site and see what Kathy Kieth is doing with Rattlesnake Press.

The poem COPPER appeared in the *Ophidian*.

The poem CAPES AND CLOTHING appeared in *Private Archaeology*, Bottle of Smoke Press, Dover, Delaware, 2013.

Special thanks to E.R. Baxter III; Tom Kryss; Bill Yates

BREAKING AND ENTERING

poetry by
D.R. WAGNER

Bob:

Once again I have to give you special thanks for all the times we shared work and spent so many hours arguing & discussing words and poems.

I am so fortunate to have you as my friend.

Don 11/13